PAYING OF TITHE: THE HISTORY BEHIND THE THEOLOGY

ROWLAND ONYENALI, CMF

TABLE OF CONTENTS

Abbreviations

ABD	Anchor Bible Dictionary
AnBib	Analecta biblica
AncB	Anchor Bible
ANT	Josephus, Antiquities of the Jews.
BCOT	Biblical Commentary on the Old Testament
BDAG	A Greek-English Lexicon of the New Testament and other Early Christian Literature
BDB	The New Brown-Driver-Briggs-Gensenius Hebrew and English Lexicon
BJRL	Bulletin of the John Rylands Library
BSC	Bible Student's Commentary Series
CBQ	Catholic biblical quarterly
Diss	Dissertation
EKK	Evangelisch-katholischer Kommentar zum Neuen Testament
EQ	Evangelical quarterly
FZAT	Forschungen zum Alten Testament
HUCA	Hebrew Union College annual
IBD	Illustrated bible dictionary
ICC	International critical commentary
IEJ	Israel exploration journal
IJCDSE	International journal for cross-disciplinary subjects in education
JBL	Journal of biblical literature
JETS	Journal of the Evangelical theological society
JS	Journal for Semites
JSOT	Journal for the study of the Old Testament
JSOT.S -	Supplement series

LNTS	Library of New Testament studies
LXX	The Septuagint
NAC	The New American commentary
NEB	Die neue Echter Bibel
NICOT	The new international commentary on the Old Testament
NIC	New international commentary
NT	Novum Testamentum
NTS	New testament studies
OTS	Oudtestamentische Studien
PTMS	Pittsburgh theological monograph series
RvEXP	Review and expositor
SBL	Society of biblical literature
SJTh	Scottish journal of theology
SNTSMS	Society for New Testament studies monograph series
SO	Studia Orientalia
STDJ	Study on the texts of the dessert of Judah
StudBL	Studies in biblical Literature
S.V.	Sub voce
TDNT	Theological dictionary of the New Testament
TDOT	Theological Dictionary of the Old Testament
TGST	Tesi Gregoriana serie teologia
TMSJ	The masters seminary journal
TNICNT	The new international commentary on the New Testament
TSBNT	The Semitic background of the New Testament
TynB	Tyndale bulletin
VT.S	Vetus Testamentum
WBC	Word biblical commentary
WGT	Wissenschaftliche Gesellschaft für Theologie
WMANT	Wissenschaftliche Monographien zum Alten und Neuen Testament

WUNT   Wissenschaftliche Untersuchungen zum Neuen
            Testament
ZAW   Zeitschrift für die alttestamentliche Wissenschaft

Foreword

Payment of tithe has received untold attention in recent years among preachers in Christian churches especially in the developing world. There is so much talk about the need to pay tithe in order to secure divine blessings in one's life. Without really taking the pains to critically investigate the rationale behind the Old Testament's injunction to pay tithes, many preachers have subscribed to it apparently because of the immediate benefits that accrue to the preachers. Wrong theologies have been propounded by many of these preachers, which tend to present a magical use of tithes. Reverend Dr. Rowland Onyenali, C.M.F., a member of Faculty at the Spiritan International School of Theology Attakwu, Enugu, in this thorough and well-researched book, addresses the issue of the payment of tithe from the perspectives of history, exegesis and theology. My journey through this book has been intellectually and spiritually rewarding.

No doubt, the overemphasis placed on tithing in many quarters today is not unconnected with the malaise of materialism. Those who benefit from the tithes are so committed to promoting it that they do not care about the soundness of their theology of tithe payment. It is surprising that many of these Christian preachers, while deemphasizing many Old Testament commands, cling tenaciously to the issue of tithe. They could care less about the fact that the Christian demand is higher, i.e., total self-giving in love, and is against any element of superstition that attempts to reduce one's offering to simply an attempt to manipulate the deity.

As the author shows, it is clear from history that tithing is an age-old practice and has continued to endure. Many ancient Near Eastern civilizations before Judaism of the Second Temple, and the Greco-Roman world practiced this. It could be regular or occasional, voluntary or commanded. It is striking that in the Old Testament tithe payment originally had to do with agricultural produce and not money and it originated in the Mosaic Law mainly as a source of sustenance for the Levites (Leviticus 27:30-33). Money came in later as a way to facilitate the offering.

The connection between tithing and divine blessings found especially in the prophet Malachy is taken too far by some preachers to the point that the ancient principle of religion that entails a trade: *do ut des*, a kind of trade by barter between gods and their adherents, is central. These preachers propagate an understanding that seems to present God as one who could be bribed with one's tithe. The author invites us to rethink this understanding. In fact, there is an overwhelming evidence of a reversed order whereby divine blessings precede tithing and not the other way round.

As one will notice in this work, an essential part of the understanding of tithe has to do with the care of ministers in God's house. In every age people are invited to care for the welfare of their religious ministers. While the payment of tithe took care of this at some point in the Old Testament, it behooves the new generations to ascertain the best way to ensure that the ministers of God's house are properly taken care of. Continuing to lay emphasis on tithe in the new dispensation, according to the author, obscures the new understanding of priesthood found in Christ. In his usual way, Onyenali has displayed in this work, so much excellence and erudition that anyone wishing to be schooled on the question of tithe today cannot afford to ignore.

Mark Enemali, C.S.Sp., PhD.

INTRODUCTION

Listen to this instructive story: When the great Rabbi Israel Baal Shem-Tov saw misfortune threatening the Jews it was his custom to go into a certain part of the forest to meditate. There he would light a fire, say a special prayer, and the miracle would be accomplished and the misfortune averted. Later, when his disciple, the celebrated Magid of Mazeritch, had occasion, for the same reason, to intercede with heaven, he would go to the same place in the forest and say, "Master of the Universe, listen! I do not know how to light the fire, but I am still able to say the prayer." And again the miracle would be accomplished. Still later, Rabbi Moshe-Leib of Sassove, in order to save his people once more, would go into the forest and say: "I do not know how to light the fire; I do not know the prayer, but I know the place and this must be sufficient." It was sufficient and the miracle was accomplished. Then it fell to Rabbi Israel of Rizhin to overcome misfortune. Sitting in his armchair, his head in his hands, he spoke to God: "I am unable to light the fire and I do not know the prayer; I cannot even find the place in the forest. All I can do is to tell the story, and this must be sufficient." And it was sufficient.[1] If this story were to continue, one might find a situation whereby the next Rabbi would even not be able to tell the story. Yet, the miracle would also be achieved. Even in the case of the absence of a Rabbi, God would still do his miracle.

There is another more instructive story. A great Zen Buddhist master, who was in charge of the Mayu Kagi monastery, had a cat which was his true passion in life. So, during meditation classes, he kept the cat by his side – in order to make the most of his company.

One morning, the master – who was already quite old – passed away. His best disciple took his place. – What shall we do with the cat? – asked the other monks. As a tribute to the memory of their old instructor, the new master decided to allow the cat to continue attending

---

[1] E. Wiesle, Gates of the Forest, viii-xii.

the Zen Buddhist classes. Some disciples from the neighboring monasteries, traveling through those parts, discovered that, in one of the region's most renowned temples, a cat took part in the meditation sessions. The story began to spread.

Many years passed. The cat died, but as the students at the monastery were so used to its presence, they soon found another cat. Meanwhile, the other temples began introducing cats in their meditation sessions: they believed the cat was truly responsible for the fame and excellence of Mayu Kagi's teaching.

A generation passed, and technical treatises began to appear about the importance of the cat in Zen meditation. A university professor developed a thesis – which was accepted by the academic community – that felines have the ability to increase human concentration, and eliminate negative energy. And so, for a whole century, the cat was considered an essential part of Zen Buddhist studies in that region.

Until a master appeared who was allergic to animal hair, and decided to remove the cat from his daily exercises with the students. There was a fierce negative reaction – but the master insisted. Since he was an excellent instructor, the students continued to make the same progress, in spite of the absence of the cat. Little by little, the monasteries – always in search of new ideas, and already tired of having to feed so many cats – began eliminating the animals from the classes. In twenty years new revolutionary theories began to appear – with very convincing titles such as "The Importance of Meditating Without a Cat", or "Balancing the Zen Universe by Will Power Alone, Without the Help of Animals".

Another century passed, and the cat withdrew completely from the meditation rituals in that region. But two hundred years were necessary for everything to return to normal – because during all this time, no one asked why the cat was there.[2]

---

[2] P. Coelho, Flowing River, 112ff.

In the human effort to understand the divine, attempts are always geared towards the establishment of clear rules and regulations of worship. These rules were meant to guide the individual worshipper and the group of worshippers towards encounter with God. As John Letts mentions, "without venturing to date the commencement, or enquiring into the *jus divinum*, of a custom so eminently remote, it will suffice to mention, that the payment of them was originally purely voluntary…"[3] In many cases, the worshippers are meant to follow these laws to the letter and any deviation might attract some punishment or reprimand depending on the level of deviation. Curiously, examples are also legion where these regulations, supposedly written on marble and thrown down from heaven have been changed in the course of time as more revelations are made on the nature of God and his demands from humans. One only needs to think of the re-interpretation of the Laws of Moses in the life of Jesus. Also there are numerous instances where the early church has reformed or totally altered the laws of the old dispensation. These alterations did not breach the relationship between God and humans; rather they enhanced it. This is the only way an old tradition can remain relevant.

The present book is focused on the issue of tithing among the Christian denominations. For the Christians, this is an old tradition originating from Judaism. Since the publication of our book *Let Our Women give Birth like the Hebrew Women* in 2014,[4] we have received many impulses to develop the issue of tithe in modern Christianity. In that book we pointed out the many *misreadings* of the Scriptures and ways in which a *discontextual* reading of any passage can lead to misinterpretations of geometric proportions. In the book also, the issue of tithing received an auxiliary view and played an ancillary role. In this

---

[3] J. Letts, A Succinct History, 1
[4] See R. Onyenali, Hebrew Women, especially pages 40-54. The issues hinted at in that book will be discussed fully and more systematically here.

volume, it forms the focus. We also showed in *Matthew's Gospel as Enculturated Narrative,* how the first gospel of the Christian canon is a product of cultural conditioning. This book which appeared in 2015 compared the gospel according to Matthew with that according to Mark, showing how the redactions found in Matthew reflect the faith of the community he was writing to.[5]

In the many attempts to justify tithing, many Christian denominations have grabbed the Old Testament by the jugulars and squeezed out many forms of theological juice from it. The books of the Torah and the prophetic utterances of Malachi form the bedrock of such teachings. This volume is a humble scholarly attempt to test the acidic nature of this theological juice against the backdrop of the origin and intentions of tithing. It is an attempt to bring out the sense of these biblical texts in the light of modern developments in the Christian world. It takes the reader from the meaning and origin of tithing in antiquity to the modern-day application of this principle. It is not meant to ruffle some ecclesial feathers or cause some rumbles in some *pastorpreneural* stomachs that might see this book as a threat. It is a historical and theological study of a thorny issue in Christendom. The words of Bright can be quoted in this connection with whole-hearted approval:

> I am not among those who feel that the historian, out of devotion to some sacred cow of objectivity, is forbidden to inject [one's] own theological convictions into his [or her] work, provided he [or she] does so at the right times and in the right way. But history and theology must be kept separate lest both historical event and theological interpretation of that event be placed on the same plane. If these two are confused, the historian will begin to

---

[5] In the preface to the book, we noted that the book is an introduction to biblical enculturation while promising that later volumes will expound the task. The publication of this book is a fulfilment of the promise. Yet, this is not the end.

write history, as it were, from the side of God, and God himself will tend to become a datum of history.[6]

For those used to reading the Hebrew bible as piece of historical reportage devoid of theological interpretation, or those who understand the inspiration of the bible to mean that the sacred book was thrown down from heaven, this enterprise might appear like the proverbial chase of the wild goose. But for those with genuine interest to understand why *the cat was there* in the first place, this book is indispensable.

---

[6] J. Bright, A History of Israel, 29- 30.

CHAPTER ONE
THE MEANING AND ORIGIN OF BIBLICAL TITHING

In responding to the meaning and origin of the practice of tithing certain questions would naturally confront the researcher. They include the following: was the tithe original to the Jewish religion or a practice bequeathed to the Jews by their pagan neighbours?[1] If it has a pagan origin, was it a form of political taxation to be paid by a vassal to an overlord? Again, if it has a religious tone under a pagan origin, could it be proof that God instituted it as an ancient practice among the pagans?[2] If the tithe has a Jewish origin, was it given as a law to be practiced unconditionally by any follower of the Abrahamic religions? Were there some historical exigencies that necessitated the payment of the tithe? Do these historical factors still exist? These are just preliminary to the main issues that would follow.

1.1 Etymology of Tithe

Despite the fact that tithes and tithing have been preached and marketed in recent times as indispensable to the worship of God, one still needs to delve into the meaning and origin of a concept of such tremendous importance. Ordinarily, the word "tithe" simply means a tenth. But a clear delimitation of the content of this tenth makes a precise definition of tithe very important. For the purpose of clarity, tithe (Heb. Piel asar, ma'aser; Gk apodekatoo) is the dedication of a tenth of agricultural

---

[1] Many liberals think that the Levitical codification of the tithe was a direct borrowing from heathen practices. See, in this connection, the following: H. Jagersma, "The Tithes in the Old Testament," in: Remembering All the Way, OTS XXI (Leiden, 1981), 116-28; Marvin E. Tate, "Tithing: Legalism or Benchmark?" RevExp 70 (Spring 1973), 153; Encyclopedia Judaica, s.v. "Tithe," by M. Weinfeld; The Interpreters Dictionary of the Bible, s.v. "Tithe," by H. H. Guthrie, Jr. Included in this group are all those who view Israel's "cultus" as evolutionary and not revelational.
[2] This seems to be the view of conservative scholars. See H. Lansdell, Sacred Tenth, 1:38.

products, of livestock, of goods gained in trade, or of booty to the worship of a deity or to the persons who served that worship.[3] It seems here that the tithe is all-embracing as it covers not only agricultural goods and livestock but also includes the gains made by traders and those involved in warfare. Since farming and trading were the main occupations of ancient climes the implication is that the content of the tithe could be all-embracing.

According to the Encyclopedia Americana, the tithe is "the tenth part of produce or other income, paid voluntarily or under the compulsion of law for the benefit of religious institutions, the support of priests and pastors, and the relief of those in need."[4] The last cited definition introduces the element of compulsion in tithing. But the two quotations agree that it has to do with the religious aspect of humans. This religious aspect seems to be evident from the OT stipulations on the tithe where it seems to have functioned as a religious tax.

Therefore, a tithe has to be seen as a tenth of the income or gain made by an individual which he/she dedicates to his god as a sort of religious tax. It could also be concluded that ordinarily it is a free offering but could be made compulsory under certain circumstances. These circumstances could include the unwillingness to carry out this religious obligation from the part of the worshipper or because of the pressing need of the particular religion. Such pressing need could involve the care of those in charge of worship and also the provision of the objects of worship in that particular religion.[5]

1.2 Origin of Tithe

The origin of tithing cannot be limited to the Jewish religion. In the words of Lansdell, "the picture-writings of Egypt, the cuneiform tablets

---

[3] A. C. Myers (ed), The Eerdmans Bible Dictionary, "Tithe," 1008.
[4] Quoted in E. K. von Russell, The Church, 6.
[5] See R. North, Eser, et al, TDOT XI.407.

of Babylon and early writers of Greece and Rome inform us that before the Bible was written, and apart therefrom, it was an almost universal practice among civilized nations for people to pay tithes to their gods; but none tell us when, or where, the practice began, or who issued the law for its observance."[6] There are tithes in pagan history that predate the Mosaic Law by centuries.[7] Some studies have it that the tithe was present in the cultures of Ugarit, Rome, Greek, Carthage, Crete, Silicia, Phonecia, China, Babylon, Egypt, etc. Ancient tithes seem to have had both a religious and political aspect. Religiously, it was connected with offerings of first fruits. Politically, it was connected with tribute and taxation.[8] The Encyclopedia of Religion reports that "in the Ancient Near East lie the origins of a sacred offering or payment of a tenth part of stated goods or property to the deity. Often given to the king or to the royal temple, the 'tenth' was usually approximate, not exact. The practice is known from Mesopotamia, Syria-Palestine, Greece and as far to the west as the Phoenician city of Carthage."[9] It is also recorded by the Westminster Dictionary of the bible that the separation of certain portion of a person's produce or spoils of war as tribute to their gods was practiced by many cultures in antiquity. It notes that "the Lydians offered a tithe of their booty… the Phoenicians and Carthaginians sent a tithe annually to the Tyrian Hercules. These tithes might be regular or occasional, voluntary or prescribed by law."[10]

In all probability, the use of the number ten has a symbolic origin, not only in Judaism but also in many other cultures. According to Hauch, its importance seems to be with the counting of the fingers of the two hands.[11] The importance of the number ten is already seen in the OT

---

[6] H. Lansdell, Sacred Tenth, 1:7.

[7] J. R. Lundbom gives a list of scholars who have studied the presence of tithe in ancient cultures in his Deuteronomy: A Commentary, 483.

[8] J. Hastings (ed), Encyclopedia of Religion and Ethics, Vol. XII "Tithes," 347.

[9] Quoted in E. K. von Russell, The Church, 6.

[10] Quoted in E. K. von Russel, The Church, 6.

where it stands for completeness as seen in the ten plagues in Egypt (Ex 7-11), in the Ten Commandments at Sinai (Ex 20; Deut 5), the Ten Patriarchs before the Flood (Gen 5), the measurements of the Ark (Gen 6:15), the Tent (Ex 26:27) and the Temple (I Kgs 6:7). This symbolic importance could have influenced the payment of a tenth of a person's agricultural income in the OT. However, when and how the tithe or tenth part became a part of cultic worship must remain an open question.

1.2.1 Tithe in Ancient Egypt

The Egyptian records predate Christianity with at least four thousand years. If one adds the pre-historic period, one realizes how ancient the Egyptian traditions are. In some of these data, the duties to the gods are reiterated. H. Lansdell, quoting F. Petrie, notes the following as some of the confessions of the faithful worshippers in the temple of Osiris: "I have not cut short the rations of the temples; I have not diminished the offerings of the gods; I have not stolen the properties of the gods."[12] These negative confessions show how the conscience of the cult faithful is highly sensitive to the duties to the temple.

With regard to the tithe proper, a Steele found at Naucratis in Egypt, dating from the first year of Nectanebo I (380 BC, the Egyptian 13th dynasty) decrees that the temple of Neith of Sais is to receive a tithe of port taxes of Naucratis.[13] This means that the tithe stretches back to the earliest written records of the human race. These tithes might be regular or occasional, voluntary or prescribed by law.[14] Some studies have shown that the tithe may be approximate and may reflect a person's status rather than an accurate measurement of the tenth of his income.[15]

---

[11] F. Hauck, "δέκα" TDNT II.36.

[12] H. Lansdell, Sacred Tenth, 1:2.

[13] Cf. M. Lichtheim, Ancient Egyptian Literature, III: 86-89; see also R. North, "Eser, et al," TDOT, XI.404ff.

[14] J. D. Davis (ed.), Westminster Dictionary of the Bible, s.v. "tithe.

[15] Cf. E. Salonen, "Ueber den Zehnten in Alten Mesopotamien," SO, XLIII:4, Helsinki

It is possible that suspicion of failure to pay the tithes prescribed by law leads to the king of profession seen above. The tithe is also connected to other forms of offering to the gods including the offering of the first fruits.[16] During the reigns of Ramses II and Ramses III the temple received about 3,220 loaves of bread, 24 cakes, 144 jugs of beer, 32 geese, and several jars of wine from the devotees.[17]

1.2.2 Tithe Around the Euphrates

When we turn our attention to the regions of the Euphrates, where the ancient Babylonians, Chaldeans and Assyrians lived, the picture is not much different. In the words of H. Lansdell, "the cuneiform inscriptions of Babylonia contain frequent references to it. It went back to the pre-Semitic age of Chaldea, and the great temples of Babylonia were largely supported by the esra of tithe which was levied upon prince and peasant alike."[18] This is based on the supposition that it is not a feat to give to the gods a tenth of what they have bestowed on humanity. Continuing, Lansdell avers that "there are many tablets in the British Museum which are receipts for the payment of the tithe to the great temple of the sun-god at Sippara, in the time of Nebuchadnezzar and his successors. From one of them we learn that Belshazzar, even at the very moment when the Babylonian Empire was falling from his father's hands, nevertheless found an opportunity for paying the tithe due from his sister."[19] Here we see the payment of an eshru, which literally means the tenth part. However, there is no agreement whether this tenth part is the tenth part of a person's income or of a person's property.[20] This eshru could be

---

(1972), 43; H. Jagersma,"The Tithes in the Old Testament," OTS XXI (1981), 116-28. Because of this, J. Baumgart advocates the non-Literal use of ma'aser/dekate in JBL 103 (1984), 245-251.

[16] Cf. A. Erman, Life in Ancient Egypt, 272.

[17] A. Erman, Life in Ancient Egypt, 277.

[18] H. Lansdell, Sacred Tenth, 1:15.

[19] H. Lansdell, Sacred Tenth, 1:15.

[20] Cf. H. Lansdell, Sacred Tenth, 1:11.

annual; it could be paid in kind maybe through some sort of labour. Also two or more individuals can combine to pay an eshru and the eshru can also be paid to a number of gods collectively.[21]

We get an insight into the payment of tithe in Chaldea during the time of Tukultiabale, better known in history as Tiglath Pileser who lavished offerings on the gods and enriched their temples with the spoils of his war.[22] After most of his expeditions he offered more than half of the spoils to the temples of his gods Asshur, Shamesh and Ramman as thanksgiving for their aid in battle.[23] If this action is taken as a norm in this area, then it furnishes a positive folio to the encounter between Abram and the priest Melchizedek which we shall see later. The major difference is that while Abram offered a tenth, Tiglat-pileser offered the greater portion of the spoils to his gods. The payment of tithes is also noted in the Arabian and Ethiopian nations. In drawing a parallelism between the Arabs and other Semitic groups, Robertson Smith, a former professor of Arabic makes the following comments: "from the Coran (sic) 137 and other sources we have sufficient evidence that the settled Arabs paid to the god a regular tribute from their fields, apparently by marking off as his a certain portion of the irrigated and the cultivated grounds."[24] However, Smith did not inform us what the situation was like with regard to the unsettled or wandering Arabs. However, one must observe that a reference to any portion of the Quran shows that we are referring to a later date and not to the ancient origin of tithe which is our concern at the moment.

1.2.3 Tithe Among the Greeks

If we turn to the religion of the Greeks we float on the realm of mythology and poetry. According to Greek writers, the events that gave

---

[21] H. Lansdell, Sacred Tenth, 1:11.
[22] H. Lansdell, Sacred Tenth,1: 13.
[23] G. Maspero, The Struggle, 659.
[24] R. Smith, Religion of the Semites, 110.

rise to tithe revolve around the period of 1300 BC, years before the Trojan War. The records have it that it was a certain Reccaranus who recovered his stolen oxen and therefore dedicated an altar in Rome probably to Jupiter calling it the greatest and teaching people to dedicate their tithes there.[25] From the rich accessories of Greek prose and poetry,[26] one sees how relevant the payment of tithes was for this culture. This is understandable in an era when the simple souls believed that all the earth and its growths were possessed by some spiritual force. In this state of affairs, to clear the ground and to sow on it was thought to be a disturbance to the original owners of the land. Hence, appropriate sacrifices and gifts were necessary to appease the spirits. Failure to pay tithes in ancient Greece was enough for a wealthy statesman to be ridiculed.[27]

There is ample evidence of the presentation of votive offerings to the Greek gods at Delphi, Sparta or even Athens.[28] During such presentations, the priest shares in the victims slaughtered.[29] In an instance, Lucian makes the god Pan complain about the neglect he suffered from the hands of his devotees. In his *Bis Accusatus* or the Double Indictment Lucian puts the following words in the mouth of Pan: "they don't treat me as I deserve at all, far worse indeed than I might have expected, when I defended them from all that barbarian garboil. However, they do come up twice or thrice in the year, with unmistakable billygoat smelling most rank; then they sacrifice him, and make a feast of the flesh, calling me witness their jollity and honouring me with a

---

[25] Cf. H. Lansdell, Sacred Tenth, 1:21-22.
[26] See for instance the Knights of Aristophanes, 300 where he mentions that the ten percent belongs to the judges.
[27] Cf. H. Lansdell, Sacred Tenth, 1:27.
[28] Cf. W. H. D. Rouse, Greek Votive Offerings: An Essay in the History of Greek Religion. Cambridge, 1902.
[29] W. H. D. Rouse, Greek Votive Offerings, 41f.

handclap or two."[30] The parallelism between the *Panan* indictment and the accusations of the biblical prophets is not to be mistaken.[31]

It might be of interest to the student of philosophy to note that the payment of tithe was noted by no less a person than Aristotle.[32] Writing about the leadership of Peisistratus, he enumerates how he aided the farmers in their cultivation of the land and how he collected tithes from the produce of the farm. A closer examination reveals that the type of tithe Aristotle mentions is a sort of tax on the farmers and not any sort of religious offering to attract the blessing of any god.

1.2.4 Tithes in Ugarit

It is possible that the tithe paid at Ugarit has the most important connection with the Hebrew tithe than any other in ancient culture. This is based on several factors: the language of Ugarit is similar to Hebrew; some Ugaritic gods like Baal and Dagon are mentioned in the Hebrew Scriptures; Ugarit was geographically closer to the land occupied by the Hebrews on entering the Promised Land than other centres of civilization in the Ancient Near East.[33] In Ugaritic and Phoenician sources, the tithe was paid as a sort of taxation to the throne. Although it was the priest that normally collected the tithe there seems to have been no religious undertone to this.[34] The priest was simply recognized as an official to the throne. Moreover, the distribution of the tithe was determined not by the priest who collected the tithe but by the political lords. The king in Ugarit gave out the tithes to his servants as a form of grant. Let us consider this text from Ugarit:

"From the present day on, Ammistamru, son of Niqmepa, king of
Ugarit has given to Yasiranu, son of Husanu, the village (alu) E[-

---

[30] Lucian, Bis Accusatus, 10.

[31] For example 1 Sam 15:22-23; Is 1:11-14; Amos 5:21-23: Micah 6:6-9; Jer 7: 21-23.

[32] Aristotle, Constitution of Athens, XVI.

[33] Cf. W. G. E. Watson/N. Wyatt (eds.), Handbook, 5.

[34] M. Heltzer, "On Tithe Paid in Grain at Ugarit," IEJ 25 (1975), 124-28.

]ish with everything it has forever, (also) to his sons and grandsons, its grain, its beer (sikaru) of its (the village's) tithe (ma'sharu), and the sheep – the pasturing tax (ma-aq-qa-du) shall be for Yasiranu. The silver of the gifts and the silver of the bridegroom's friend and service boys (su-sa-pi-in-nu-ti) shall be for Yasiranu."[35]

That was the official way of handling the tithe in Ugarit. One easily notices the linguistic closeness between the Hebrew ma'aser and the ma'sharu of Ugarit. In Ugarit, the temple was subsidiary to the throne and could thus not exact any influence on the tithe. This is quite different from what we shall see in the case of Mosaic legislation on tithes. It is also different from the current practice where the tithe is paid to religious leaders and not to the political heads. There are instances in Ugarit where the temple officials are explicitly barred from interfering with tithes. An example is found in the following text:

"From the present day Niqmadu, son of Ammistamru king of Ugarit gave (donated) the village Uhnappu to Kar-Kushuh, son of Ana[nu] and to Apapa, the king's daughter, with its tithe ('shr) with its custom-duties (miksu). Nobody shall raise claims concerning Uhnappu against Kar-Kushuh and Apapa and against the sons of Apapa. He (the king) donated Uhnappu. Further: Kar-Kushuh is pure like the sun forever. Later he is (also) pure. The temple of Ba'al of the Hazi mountain and its priests shall not have claims to Kar-Kushuh."[36]

The above text shows that the tithe is seen from the perspective of a whole village.[37] In places where tithes were paid to Baal, the Ugaritic

---

[35] W. W. Hallo, Context of Scripture I-III, 258.
[36] W. W. Hallo, Context of Scripture I-III, 201.
[37] See G. A. Anderson, Sacrifices and offerings, 79.

god, it was a bid to employ the aid of Baal to repel the attacks of an enemy. This implies that such tithes were spontaneous and not the normal routine. In a religious text from Ugarit, the tither partook of it in a sacrificial banquet; this depicts the provision of the Deuteronomic code (Deut 14:22-26).[38] In Ugarit, the tithe was seen as a royal tax which the king received from the people for himself and for the benefit of his officials

As said above, the subsidiary position of the temple relative to the throne makes the reception and distribution of tithes the prerogative of the king. This seems to have left some vestiges in the Hebrew Scriptures. Samuel warned the Israelites that the king they are asking for would demand a tenth of all their belongings from them (I Sam 8:15-17). Following this line of thought, during the days of King Hezekiah's reforms, he imposed the tithe on his subjects. Although it was ordered by the king, it was for the use of the Temple ministers so that they could devote themselves to the Law of the Lord (II Chron. 31:4). In response, the people of Judah brought it in abundance and the quantity was so great that special chambers had to be built in the Temple to contain them (II Chron. 31: 11). The importance of this kind of chamber for the tithes would be seen later (→ 4.4).

1.2.5 Booty of War in Antiquity

What is to be done with the booty of war in some cultures of antiquity is well documented by many historians.[39] It appeared all too normal that the victorious party in the war offers some part of the booty to his god as sign of gratitude for victory gained. This is in recognition that no victory

---

[38] Cf. H. Jagersma, "The Tithes in the Old Testament," 118.

[39] W. H. D. Rouse, in his Greek Votive Offerings, 102 documents that "there are dedications of the war-tithe at Apollonia, Athens, Branchidai, Crete, Mantinea, Megara, Boetia, and Sparta; at Delphi by Athenians, Caphyes, Cnidians, Liparians, Spartans, and Tarentines; at Olympia by Cleitorians, Eleans, Messenians, Spartans, Thurians."

was possible without the intervention of the gods. As W. K. Pritchett notes with regard to the Greek state, "of all places in Greece, Olympia…offers rich evidence for the custom of making offerings in recognition of benefits bestowed in the temple where dwelt the mighty dispenser of victory, Zeus."[40] This view is concretized by Thucydides (born 471 BC) who tells us that when the Athenians divided the land of Lesbos into three thousand portions, they consecrated a tithe of it to the gods.[41] For instance, Herodotus, the father of history has presented some documents of the payment of the Dekate in cases of war that could serve as blue print for the actions of Abram in Gen 14. He notes of the Phoceans after the victory over the Thesalians:

> "Having brought all the loot together, they set apart a tithe for the god of Delphi. From this was made and dedicated that tripod which rests upon the bronze three-headed serpent, nearest to the altar; another they set apart for the god of Olympia, from which was made and dedicated a bronze figure of Zeus, ten cubits high; and another for the god of the Isthmus, from which was fashioned a bronze Poseidon seven cubits high. When they had set all this apart, they divided what remained, and each received, according to his worth, concubines of the Persians and gold and silver, and all the rest of the stuff and the beasts of burden."[42]

The practice of dedicating spoils of war to the gods seems to have been recognized by historians of late antiquity. Pausanias (c. AD 110- c. 180) a Greek traveler and geographer of the 2nd century AD notes that after the Lakedaimonians defeated the Athenians at Tanagra, they made a golden shield out of the spoils they had taken from the Argives, Athenians and Ionians and sent it to Olympia where it hung on the gable

---

[40] W. K. Pritchett, The Greek State at War, 95.
[41] Cf. H. Lansdell, Sacred Tenth, 1:27.
[42] Herodotus Histories 9.81.1, quoted in L. L. Brice, Greek Warfare, 223f.

of the temple of Zeus just below the status of Nike.[43] The few examples above show that the dedication of spoils of war to gods was an ancient practice. It could be one of the many reasons that motivated nations to engage in warfare. It is not surprising that the powerful nations eventually became the wealthiest nations.

We also have information about the various things that could constitute the war tithe. It could include slaves, land or money. For example, a train of maidens was taken when Oichalia was destroyed. This is reported in Sophocles Trachiniai.[44] In his report Sophocles employs ἐξελέσθαι (exelesthai) which is a technical term for the chosen spoils allotted to the generals.[45] A tithe of slaves is also mentioned in Athens.[46] We have already mentioned how the Athenians divided the land of Lesbos. This is evidence of the use of land as tithe. In 394 BC Agesilaos dedicated a hundred Talents of Gold, derived from the war spoils of his campaign in Asia Minor to Delphi.[47] This is example of the use of money to settle the obligation of the war dekate. It is possible that the sharing of the remnant among the men of valour who took part in the warfare was also a universal custom among ancient cultures.

Fortunately, the biblical records also present us with a blueprint of Israel's dealings with the spoils of war. We shall see this later (3.4). A cursory reading of the OT also shows how defeat in battle led to subjugation of a nation or the paying of taxes to the victor (cf. 2 Kgs 15:20). However, we have rich information concerning the dealings between Judah and Assyria. Hezekiah's tribute to Sennachrib is extant in a lengthy bull said to have been preserved *in situ* by archeologists. This bull contains interesting remarks which are worth quoting here:

---

[43] Cf. W. K. Pritchett, The Greek State at War, 95.

[44] Sophocles, Trachiniai, 244-245.

[45] In Acts 7:34 it refers to the deliverance of the Israelites from bondage in Egypt.

[46] Cf. W. K. Pritchett, The Greek State at War, 96.

[47] Cf. W. K. Pritchett, The Greek State at War, 96.

I drew near to Ekron- the governors who had rebelled (committed sin) I slew with the sword. The citizens who had rebelled (sinned) I counted as spoil. The rest of them, who had not rebelled, I pardoned. Padi, their king, I brought out of Jerusalem and placed on the throne over them. My royal tribute I imposed upon him. As for Hezekiah, the Jew, who had not submitted to my yoke, 46 of his strong, walled cities and the cities of their environs, which were numberless, I besieged, I captured, I plundered, as booty I counted. Him, like a caged bird in Jerusalem, his royal city, I shut up. Earth works I threw up about it. His cities which I plundered, I cut off from his land and gave to the kings of Ashdod, Askelon, Ekron and Gaza-I diminished his land. To the former tribute, I imposed and laid upon him the giving up of his land as a gift. That Hezekiah,- the terrifying splendor of my royalty overcame him, and the Arabs and the picked troops whom he had brought into Jerusalem, his royal city, ran away. With 30 talents of gold, 800 talents of silver and all kinds of treasure from his palace, he sent his daughters, his palace women, his male and female singers, to Nineveh, and he dispatched his messenger to pay the tribute"[48]

Curiously, the bull of Sennachrib bears much resemblance to the record of the Jewish scriptures. We read the following words:

In the fourteenth year of King Hezekiah's reign, Sennacherib king of Assyria attacked all the fortified cities of Judah and captured them. So Hezekiah king of Judah sent this message to the king of Assyria at Lachish: "I have done wrong. Withdraw from me, and I will pay whatever you demand of me." The king of Assyria exacted from Hezekiah king of Judah three hundred talents of silver and thirty talents of gold. So Hezekiah gave him all the silver that was found in the temple of the Lord and in the treasuries of the royal palace. At this time Hezekiah king of Judah stripped off the gold with which he had covered the doors and doorposts of the temple of the Lord, and gave it to the king of Assyria (2 Kgs 18:13-16).

There are difficult confessions in this biblical text to make us regard it as indisputable part of actual history. The first is the Kyrie of Hezekiah. In v.14 the Jewish king makes a confession to a pagan king that is a normal confession to Yahweh (I have sinned). Again, that the biblical narrator and the final redactors allowed the stripping of the gold of the doorposts of the temple so as to pay homage to the Assyrian king (v.16) to remain in the final redaction of the text is remarkable. In as much as the bull may not represent the actual historical event it tries to describe, there is nothing in this text or in the biblical record to suggest that the vanquished nation paid a tenth of its property or income to the victorious party.[49] The ancient practice seemed to be that the overcomer laid a certain amount of tax on the vanquished enemy as tribute of acknowledgement of defeat.

In late antiquity we have records about booty collected in warfare. Most of the information is provided by Procopius in his History of the Wars.[50] In his book, most of the booty captured seemed to be for the benefit of the royal court or the state as a whole. A. D. Lee has shown the economic impact of war in late antiquity indicating how defeat in

---

[49] The use of war spoils in the scrolls of the Qumran community has been analyzed by Y. Yadin, Temple Scroll I.358-62; L. H. Schiffman, "The Laws of War in the Temple Scroll," RevQ 13 (1988), 304-6; L. H. Schiffman, "Priestly and Levitical Gifts," Provo International Conference, 485.

[50] Procopius, History of the Wars, Books V. and VI, with English translation by H.B. Dewing. Release Date: January 6, 2007 [EBook #20298]. Analysis of the information in this book has been made by A. D. Lee, War in Late Antiquity: A Social History, especially pages.101-120.

war affected cities like Thrace and the Danube, Northern Mesopotamia and Syria, Northern Gaul and Italy.[51]

1.3 Is Genesis 4:3-7 A Prelude to Biblical Tithe?

Nonetheless, there is a certain neglected episode in the book of Genesis to which some scholars have pointed as the first payment of tithe in the Jewish Scriptures. The text is Genesis 4:3-7 and the story is that of Cain and Abel.[52] This text is important since it is the first biblical record of the presentation of any form of offering to God. It also contains the interesting fact of the acceptance and rejection of offering by God. It could thus function as litmus test to the importance of any kind of gifts to the deity in the Jewish religion. The text under consideration runs thus:

> Time passed and Cain brought some of the produce of the soil as an offering for Yahweh, while Abel for his part brought the first-born of his flock and some of their fat as well. Yahweh looked with favour on Abel and his offering. But he did not look with favour on Cain and his offering, and Cain was very angry and downcast. Yahweh asked Cain; 'Why are you angry and downcast? If you are doing right, surely you ought to hold your head high! But if you are not doing right, sin is crouching at the door hungry to get you. You can still master him (Gen 4:3-7).

---

[51] A. D. Lee, War in Late Antiquity: A Social History, especially pages 101-120.

[52] Any attempt to understand the personalities or theological importance of Cain and Abel based on the teachings of Jewish rabbis in antiquity is a very subversive venture. Rabbi Eliezer and Targum Pseudo Jonathan teach that Cain was the product of Eve and the serpent. Other traditions teach that Cain and Abel were born with twin sisters. This could be a rational way of explaining the subsequent multiplication of mankind. Early Christian "exegesis" did not fail in adding to the confusion through fantastic analysis of the Cain and Abel saga. For analysis of these rabbinic and Christian teachings, see The Book of Genesis in Late Antiquity: Encounters between Jewish and Christian Exegesis, by E. Grypeou/H. Spurling, 99-145.

The biblical passage above, which is surely an interpolation,[53] appears innocent and unrelated to tithe. In this terse narrative, the boys were no sooner born than they grew into men with their respective occupations of farming and animal husbandry. They presented offerings to God. The word used to describe the sacrifices of the brothers is a hiphil form of bô, a verb that is by no means limited to sacrificial contexts but occurs too often in them to need listing.[54] That of Abel was accepted while that of Cain was rejected. The narrator presented no reason for the offerings made by the brothers. And no reason is given in the text for the divine rejection of the offering of Cain. Could the narrative be a piece of polemic against the pagan custom of offering the fruit of the land instead of the Jewish custom of offering an animal?[55] Although Israel pursued pastoral life almost throughout the Pentateuch, this does not justify Gunkel's conclusion that "Yahweh loves the shepherd and animal sacrifice, but wants nothing to do with the farmer and fruit offerings."[56] However, the Hebrew narrative uses two key words describing Abel's offering not found concerning Cain's offering of fruit of the ground. They are "firstlings" (bëkorôt; cf. Exod 34:19; Deut 12:6; 14:23) and "fat" (hëleb; cf. Num 18:17).[57] These are significant words in later Torah sacrificial instructions.[58]

---

[53] It is evident that the fourth chapter of Genesis interrupts the flow of the story of origins from chapter three to five.

[54] H. D. Preuss, "bô," TDOT II.25.

[55] This suggestion has been fronted by C. A. Simpson, Genesis, The Interpreters Bible, 518; S. Levin, "The More Savory Offering: A Key to the Problem of Gen 4:3-5," JBL 98 (1975), 85; J. Skinner, Genesis, 106. For R. S. Candlish, God's displeasure with Cain's offering stemmed from his failure to give a blood sacrifice. R. S. Candlish, An Exposition of Genesis, 65. He sees the connection with sin in the phrase 'sin is crouching at the door.'

[56] H. Gunkel, Genesis, 43.

[57] J. P. Lewis, "The Offering of Abel (Gen 4:4): A History of Interpretation," JETS 37/4 (December 1994) 481.

[58] See also G. J. Wenham, WBC vol. I (Genesis 1-15), 103.

But some conservative scholars have provided an alternative reading to this text and have tried to see it as the primordial proof text for this ancient practice of tithing. The crux of the text is v. 7[59] with the word lappetah (at the entrance or at the door). Here, it is a warning to Cain that sin is lurking at the entrance and is trying to take hold of him. Curiously, the LXX of v. 7 seems to reflect the Hebrew lenattah (to divide). It reads: Is it not so? If you offer rightly, but do not cut in pieces rightly, you have sinned? Be still! This translation identifies that the sin of Cain was the inability to divide or dissect well the offerings he was making to God. What then is he dividing if not his tithes? As early as the third century, Tertullian, commenting from the Vulgate, which is the Latin translation from the LXX, argued that God rejected the sacrifice of Cain because he did not rightly divide what he offered.[60] A look into an attempt at explaining this OT epic in the letter to the Hebrews seems to confirm this interpretation. The reader should bear in mind that the LXX was the version of the OT often cited by the Christian writers. This version must have been present to the writer of the letter to the Hebrews in composing his text. Therefore, looking at Gen 4:7, the author writes in Hebrews 11:4 that in faith Abel offered God more abundant offering than Cain. The two operative concepts here are 'faith' and 'more abundant offering.' This means that Cain was not able to offer the required percentage to God. This percentage could be a reference to the payment of his tithe. Again, faith is related to obedience. This means that if Abel offered in faith, it must be reference to a command. Where there is no law there would be no transgression of the law.[61] It is also to be argued that this command must have been known to the two worshippers if it was the basis of the rejection of Cain's offering.

---

[59] For the history of the interpretation of this verse, see G. J. Wenham, Genesis, WBC, vol. I (Gen 1-15), 104-106. See also J. P. Lewis, "The Offering of Abel (Gen 4:4): A History of Interpretation," JETS 37/4 (December 1994) 481-496.

[60] Tertullian, Answer to the Jews, 2.

[61] This point has also been made by H. Landsell, Sacred Tenth, 1:10.

Therefore, it was because of this inadequate payment that his offering was not acceptable. Since the issue of faith or faithfulness to divine injunction is now in view, it can be related to the issue of righteousness.[62] Many ancient and modern commentators are of the view that while Cain was the unrighteous one, Abel was the righteous one.[63] The fact that the many ancient commentators saw Cain as having an evil origin helped to accentuate this view and to explain why his sacrifice was rejected.[64]

But we will be quick to correct that the word (pleiona) translated "abundant" in Heb 11:4 includes in its range of meaning both the qualitative idea of excellence and the quantitative idea of abundance.[65] But judging from what we understand from the Scriptures about God's appreciation of the offerings of men/women, we have to join the host of many scholars in accepting that what is at stake here is a critique of the offering of Cain based not on quantity but on the offering itself. The problem here could be the content of the offering. In this case, what is at stake is a Jewish critique of the bloodless sacrifice presented by the other nations.[66] This is an interpretation based on a consideration of the Hebrew text of the passage and not the LXX version. Hence, if the sin of Cain was based on a failure to adhere to a divine command, the Hebrew text would have made this explicit.

This is surely one of the many ways bible teachers have tried to squeeze something titheable from a host of episodes in the bible.[67]

---

[62] On the other hand, the Apocryphon of John informs us that Cain was unrighteous while Abel was righteous. Cf. Ap. John II, 24, 16-25.

[63] For the analysis of this narrative among Jewish scholars see J. P. Lewis, "The Offering of Abel (Gen 4:4): A History of Interpretation," JETS 37/4 (December 1994) 482-485.

[64] Cf. 1 John 3:10-12; Tertullian, Patience 5:15; Targum of Pseudo Jonathan Gen

[65] Cf. F. W. Danker, et al, BDAG, 689.

[66] Although we are not told that the two brothers offered a sacrifice for their sins, the offering of animals became the classical mode of sacrifice for expiation in the OT. Even the book of Hebrews asserts that without the shedding of blood there is no forgiveness of sin (Heb 9:22).

[67] See H. Lansdell, Sacred Tenth, 1:40-41.

Happily, informed scholars have followed the Hebrew text of the bible without even turning an eye to the LXX translation.[68] The influence of the LXX rendering of the verse shows the importance of translation on exegesis.[69] Even many of those scholars who have provided us with alternative translations for this verse entirely fail to consider the rendering of the LXX.[70] In fact, the only way to understand the meaning of the offering is to understand the term employed in the text. The Hebrew word (minchah) generally means a gift or a present. In many places in the OT it is used for a bloodless sacrifice.[71] It seems to be the standard term used in the Levitical code for the meal offering. However, it is also frequently associated with payment of tribute or taxes.[72] For this reason, it may be suggested that Cain and Abel's gifts were mandatory. However, it can also be used as an expression of respect, thanksgiving, homage, and friendship which do not always imply obligation.[73] One is then led to conclude that the offering of the two brothers was a kind of free offering to the deity.

Granted that the brothers did not act out of a divine mandate to offer something to God, there must still be some reasons to warrant such an

---

[68] E. A. Speiser, Genesis, (2nd ed.), 32. Most commentators follow the MT without even entertaining the LXX reading in their discussions (e.g., S. R. Driver, The Book of Genesis, 65; Franz Delitzsch, A New Commentary on Genesis (2 vols.), 181-83; V. P. Hamilton, The Book of Genesis (2 vols.), 1:225-226.

[69] A celebrated Jewish poet, Haim NachmannBialik (1873-1934) remarks that reading the bible in translation is like kissing a new bride through the veil. It also reminds the reader of an ancient Latin saying, traduttore, traditore, which implies that a translator is like a traitor. Had the LXX not used the words 'divide rightly' for Gen 4:7, the history of the interpretation of this passage would have been much different.

[70] C. Westermann gives an otherwise complete list of philological options for the verse, but does not view the LXX reading as worthy of mention. See his Genesis (3 vols.), Continental Commentaries, 1:299-301).

[71] Cf. Genesis 32:14; Genesis 32:19; Genesis 32:21; Genesis 32:22 (E), Genesis 33:10; Genesis 43:11,15,25,26 (J), Judges 6:18; 1 Samuel 10:27; 1 Kings 10:25 2Chronicles 9:24; 2 Kings 8:8,9; 2 Kings 20:12 = Isaiah 39:1; Psalm 45:13; 2Chronicles 32:23.

[72] See Gen 32:13; Jdg 3:15.17f; 1 Sam 10:27.

[73] Cf. G. B. Gray, Sacrifice in the Old Testament, 16-17

action. We have already argued that God's rejection of Cain's offering was not quantitatively based. In the same way, it seems improbable that the offering was rejected on the grounds of qualitative inadequacy. First, it would be difficult to argue that Cain offered unclean beasts since the distinction between clean and unclean was introduced afterwards (cf. Gen 7:8). Second, although some scholars have tried to contrast the fat and firstborn elements of Abel's sacrifice with the mere 'some' of Cain's fruits and vegetables,[74] one has to accept that since the only argument that is given in the text for the acceptance of the one and the rejection of the other is from the silence of the narrative, every other scholarly input on this text is a matter of conjecture. As already said, if we have recourse to the NT explanation, we conclude that it was a matter of faith and lack of it. According to Heb 11:4 it was because of Abel's faith that his offering was more acceptable than that of his brother. More cannot be said on this with certainty. But we can conclude with certainty that from the earliest written Jewish history, men have sought ways of bringing offerings to God from the abundance of their produce. This is the case with Noah, Abraham, Isaac and Jacob. And from other ancient cultures, there was this custom of not eating the first fruits of farm and animals without setting aside a certain percentage for the deity. This is what Cain and Abel could have done. We can also conclude that there is no link whatsoever between this episode and the Levitical tithe that would be codified centuries later.

Having seen that the offering of Cain and Abel is not related to tithe, we have to look elsewhere in the OT for the origin of tithe. Attention naturally falls on the tenth paid by Abram to Melchizedek. It is in this portion of the bible that the terminology was used for the first time. However, this episode is so important that it deserves an entire chapter.

---

[74] Cf. also F. Delitzsch, Genesis, 180-81; H. Gunkel, Genesis, 42-43; A. P. Ross, Creation & Blessing, 157-158; K. A. Matthews, Genesis 1:1-11:26 (NAC), 267-268

1.4 Other OT Tithes

Apart from the offering of Cain and Abel, and the tithe of Abram, to which we shall return later, there are other pre-Mosaic passages that point to the payment of tithe in the Scriptures. Consider Genesis 28:20-22. In this passage, Jacob contemplates the payment of tithe to God on condition that God delivers him from his enemies. The context of this promise is easy to understand. After deceiving his father, Isaac and stealing the birthright of his elder brother Esau, and because of Esau's intent of killing him, Jacob ran away to sojourn with his uncle Laban. In the course of this journey, Jacob had a dream in which he saw a ladder that led up to heaven, with angels ascending and descending. After waking up from sleep, he erected an altar, offered sacrifice and vowed to make Yahweh his God and to give Yahweh the tenth part of all his possession if Elohim[75] spares him and provides for his needs in all his endeavours. In as much as the context of this vow is simple, the theological motif is difficult to understand. It is to be wondered why Jacob would make a conditional vow to God when God himself had already pronounced the promise (Gen. 28:13-16). The sheer brazenness of a mortal giving God conditions for the keeping of a covenant makes one to ask whether Jacob was not questioning the sovereignty of God.

Be that as it may, this narrative indicates that Jacob was aware of the payment of tithe. But since this tithe was a conditional one, it has to be accepted that it is not based on the following of any laid-down stipulation. It is possible that the issue of tithing on this occasion was based on personal disposition and cannot serve the basis for any

---

[75] The combination of Yahweh and Elohim in this passage has led some scholars to see a Canaanite influence in the Jacob's story. See for instance G. Riedl, Model Assisi, 103; Oswald Loretz, Ugarit und die Bibel. Kanaanäische Götter und Religion im Alten Testament, Darmstadt, 1990; G. J. Brooke, Ugarit and the Bible (UBL 11), Münster, 1994. The overwhelming usage of El in Ugarit texts has been investigated by M. H. Pope, El in the Ugaritic Texts, Leiden, 1955. He found out that the Ugaritic texts bear witness that El was the specific name of a god in the Semitic world.

theological treatise on tithing. That means the Jacob saga is neither normative nor foundational for the principle of tithing.

As the narrative progresses, one realizes that God blessed the days of Jacob and spared his life. But there is no indication that Jacob fulfilled his part of giving God a tithe of his possession.[76] Rather, what one reads is that on his return journey from Laban's house, after acquiring much possession, and with much fear about the possible attack by his brother Esau, Jacob had another dream. This time instead of a vision of the angels of God ascending and descending, he had to wrestle the whole night.

Finally, when Joseph was in Egypt, he used a combination of divine favour and Jewish wisdom to gain the favour of Pharaoh and save Egypt from famine. His address to the Egyptians in Genesis 47:23f is instructive. He required the people to pay a fifth of their proceeds to Pharaoh. He did not reserve anything for the priests. This was mainly because the priests produced enough food, hence no tithes were specially set aside for them (Gen 47:22.26). As already explained, tithing was in practice in ancient Egypt before the time of Joseph. This means that if Joseph was following any law, then the law of tithing might be different in Egypt or that circumstances have changed the manner of the payment of tithes.

1.5 Summary of Findings

In this first chapter, we have been able to isolate the meaning and extant beginnings of the principle of tithing in ancient and biblical cultures. The extensive research on tithe in various cultural milieus in this chapter has shown that tithe was a living practice in many cultures. Of particular

---

[76] On the other hand, stories around Jacob show his tendency to deceive. In fact, deception is the meaning of his name. The story concerning Dinah and Schechem (cf. Gen 34) show how the sons of Jacob have followed the footsteps of their father. The father-son resemblance is manifest in many OT sagas. This is evident in Abraham-Isaac (Gen 20/26); David-Solomon (1 Chron 3/1 Kgs11:3), etc.

importance is the issue of dealing with the spoils of war. The importance of the findings would become evident in later chapters. We also tried our best to locate the beginning of OT tithing in the Cain and Abel saga. But an open minded reading of our exposition would reveal that we failed to find any element of tithing from any of these brothers. Theirs was an offering from the first fruits of their fields and cattle. We have also seen that tithes were not only paid to religious leaders. In fact, it seems that tithe originated from the political set-up as a form of taxation to the throne. The OT retains a vestige of this practice in the case of the tithe recommended by Joseph in Egypt. This tithe was to be paid to the coffers of the Pharaoh while the priests were to get nothing. The essence of the tithe was to take care of the coming days of famine. So far, we are yet to see any command to tithe in the Jewish Scriptures. What Jacob did was a voluntary vow to tithe which he may not have fulfilled. But this is just the beginning because there are numerous biblical assertions and allusions that support the practice of tithing. We shall take our time to study them.

Questions to the reader: without any official representative of God (priest or king) how could Jacob have fulfilled his vow of offering a tithe of all his possession to God?

CHAPTER TWO
THE TITHE OF ABRAM (Gen 14:17-24)

The passage of Abram's warfare and payment of tithe is an obscure narrative sandwiched between the call of Abram in Genesis 12 and the triad of covenants between him and God in Genesis 15, 17 and 22. Although many biblical scholars have challenged the historicity of the Abrahamic tradition,[1] it still serves as concrete basis for the faith of the Abrahamic religions. An understanding of the text and context of Abram's tithe to Melchizedek is indispensable to an understanding of the theology of tithe which has been adopted by the followers of Christ. Bearing in mind the findings of the previous chapter, this chapter easily serves as follow up to the practice of tithe in ancient cultures.

2.1 The Context and Text of Gen 14:17-24

An understanding of the tithe paid by Abram to Melchizedek requires a grasp of the narrative that forms the crust of the event. The whole episode began when the four kings of Shinar, Ellasar, Elam and Goiim made war against the five kings of the smaller states of Sodom, Gomorrah, Admah, Zeboiim and Zoar near the Salt Sea. These five kings revolted because for about twelve years they have been under the yoke of Chedor-Laomer, the king of Elam. As was and is still normal with despots, the king of Elam rallied forces with which to crush the recalcitrant cities. Before the encounter with the four kingdoms already mentioned, he crushed nearby nations until battle was engaged against the four kings at the Valley of Siddim. While three kings escaped from the onslaught of Chedor-Laomer, the kings of Sodom and Gomorrah were not as lucky as they fell into the bitumen wells in the valley. Their

---

[1] For Van Seters, the Abrahamic tradition as it stands reflects "only a late date of composition and gives no hint by its content of any great antiquity in terms of biblical history." See V. Seters, Abraham in History and Tradition, 121-122.

39

possessions were captured as booty. Lot, who was living in the city of Sodom was taken as part of the booty (Gen 14:1-12).

It is in this connection that we understand the actions of Abram. When he was informed of the fate of his nephew, Lot, he summoned 318 men from his household and gave the four kings a hot chase. Battle was engaged in Dan. Abram won the victory and recovered everything that was captured by the kings, including Lot and all his possessions. He also returned with the other captives, and with a large amount of spoil that was taken from the Eastern kings (Gen 14:16f) against whom he fought. Abram then met Melchizedek, the priest of the Most High, and gave him a tenth of the spoil (Gen 14:20). Yes, he gave the priest a tithe of everything he captured. The remainder of the captured goods was given to the king of Sodom (Gen 14:21-24). One might wonder how Abram gave the bulk of his booty to the king of SODOM.[2] But that was exactly what he did because he would not want the king to think that Abram became rich because of the wealth of such military campaign. The narrative implies that Abram went home with nothing.

Although we have proposed to study the whole episode of the three wars and the subsequent encounter between Abram and Melchizedek, we shall here present the text of the actual encounter of Abram and Melchizedek after the wars. It is in this pericope that we read of the payment of tithe:

> When Abram returned from defeating Chedorlaomer and the kings who had been on his side, the king of Sodom came to meet him in the Valley of Shaveh (that is, the Valley of the King). Melchizedek king of Salem brought bread and wine; he was a priest of God Most High. He pronounced this blessing: Blessed be Abram by God Most High, Creator of heaven and earth. And

---

[2] We discover a beautiful sandwiching of Abram between the kings of Salem and Sodom. One could also see the refusal of Abram to go home with any of the spoils as his total trust in God as the source of his victory. This argument is concretized in Gen 15 which opens with God's promising Abram: I am your great reward.

blessed be God Most High for putting your enemies into your clutches. And Abram gave him a tenth of everything. The king of Sodom said to Abram, 'Give me the people and take the possessions for yourself.' But Abram replied to the king of Sodom, 'I swear by God Most High, Creator of heaven and earth; not one thread, not one sandal strap, will I take of what is yours, for you to be able to say, "I made Abram rich." For myself, nothing-except what the troops have used up, and the share due to the men who came with me, Eshcol, Aner and Mamre; let them take their share' (Gen 14:17-24).

It must be accepted that this text is important because it employs the technical term (maáSër) for tithe. And as already said, it is the first occurrence of the word in the whole Jewish bible. We thus have the most promising data and rich fount for this phenomenon in the OT. This pericope together with its immediate context of Genesis 14:1-16 therefore requires some level of deeper scrutiny.

2.2 The Structure

This text is one of the most controversial pericopes in the entire Pentateuch.[3] Its isolated nature has made some scholars to argue that it belongs to none of the main documents of the Hexateuch.[4] But there are also numerous voices that ascribe it to the J source.[5] It is only here in Genesis that we have an account of military expedition involving many kings.[6] It also seems to be the first instance of the glorification of war in the OT. It seems to be a pointer of what would later characterize the history of the Jews.

---

[3] Cf. J. Scharbert, NEB, Genesis 12-50, 132.
[4] Cf. H. Gunkel, Genesis, 288-290.
[5] For such voices, see G. J. Wenham, WBC, Vol. 1 (Gen 1-15), 306.
[6] G. J. Wenham, WBC, Vol. 1 (Gen 1-15), 304.

A closer look at the narrative reveals that the material is clearly divided into two main sections, namely, vv.1-16 and vv.17-24. The first section contains three accounts of battle while the second section reports the encounter between Abram and the king of Sodom with an interlude involving Melchizedek. The structure appears thus:[7]

Vv.1-16 contain three battle reports:

1-4   Eastern kings vs Western Kings: round 1

5-12   Eastern kings vs Western Kings: round 2

13-16   Abram vs Eastern Kings

Vv.17-24 contain four sub-sections:

17   King of Sodom meets Abram

18-20   Melchizedek encounters Abram

21   King of Sodom's demand

22-24   Abram's reply

The three reports of battle seem to conform to the regular convention of *regel de tri* or rule of three in Jewish historiography, that is, the peculiarity of telling a story in three scenes. That means that triadic patterns are a beloved aspect of Jewish narratology. U. Luz has noted that "…it is only a literary systematizing principle, one which is frequent in oral instruction."[8] In the first battle, Chedorlaomer and his allies defeat the king of Sodom and his allies.[9] In the second battle, Chedorlaomer and his allies again defeat several cities of Canaan. But in the third campaign Abram and his household show their superior power over the all-conquering despot, defeating him and rescuing Lot and all

---

[7] These divisions have been made by G. J. Wenham, WBC, Vol. 1 (Gen 1-15), 304

[8] U. Luz, Matthew 1-7, 38. See also R. Onyenali, Trilogy, 201f; R. Onyenali, Enculturated Narrative, 125f.

[9] There are efforts to relate the names of Chedorlaomer and his allies to some known kings during the time of Abraham. But such efforts have not yielded any positive results. See J. Scharbert, NEB, Genesis, 12-50, 133.

the other captives. It is then evident that the entrance of Abram into the story changed the contours of the whole narrative.[10]

In the second part of the narrative, Abram encounters the king of Sodom and the priest-king of Salem. It could be that the king of Sodom and his allies went to appreciate Abram for his role in defeating their enemies for them. Their gratitude is expressed in the double blessing pronounced by Melchizedek. First he blesses El Elyon and secondly blesses Abram in the name of El Elyon.[11] The identification of Melchizedek as priest of the Most High and his bringing out of bread and wine suggest that his action is connected to his office. As Scott Hahn puts it, "the proximity of Melchizedek's bringing out bread and wine, on the one hand, and the mention of his priesthood on the other suggests a connection between what is brought out and his office as priest."[12] This implies that the bread and wine are to be seen as serving both the needs of refreshment and sacrifice at the same time. The comments of Westermann seem to connect the sacred and the secular in the action of Melchizedek. He argues thus:

> "it is an event in which the secular and the sacred are still not separated. Melchizedek brings refreshment to the exhausted liberator and thus as royal host receives him into the peace, the shalom of his royal domain; but the hands that bring the bread and wine are the hands of the priest, and the food and drink are not to be separated from the blessing which Melchizedek dispenses to Abraham in the name of his God."[13]

---

[10] There could be a theological motif behind this war expedition. In the words of Steinmetz, "when Abraham enters the story, the relationship shifts to that described in Chapter 11. Abraham, the descendant of the chosen line of Shem, conquers the rest of the descendants of Noah. He asserts his ascendancy over Canaan, of course, by conquering their conquerors." D. Steinmetz, From Father to Son, 146.

[11] Cf. R. North, "eser, sr, ma'aser," TDOT, Vol. XI, 406.

[12] S. Hahn, Kingship by Covenant, 131.

[13] Quoted in S. Hahn, Kingship by Covenant, 131.

After this blessing, Abram renders a tithe of all the booty from the war.[14] What Abram offered Melchizedek could include prisoners he has taken from the war as well as other material spoils (cf. v.21). This drew the intervention of the king of Sodom who proposed a better way of sharing the booty. For the king of Sodom, Abram should give him the nepeš (that is the human spoils) and keep the goods for himself. His request was refashioned by Abram who vowed taking just a little of the spoils for his men while probably leaving with nothing. This could imply that all the figures mentioned in this part of the narrative (Melchizedek, Abram and the king of Sodom) understood the concept of sharing the booty of war, albeit differently. What Abram retained for his men could have been used for a ritual meal.[15] The paying of the tithe by Abram and the swearing in the name of El Elyon (14:22)[16] imply that Abram has pledged loyalty to Melchizedek and the god he serves.

However, various elements of the text point to its unhistorical nature. They include: (a) the circuitous route the five kings took to quench the revolt; (b) the presentation that Abram had a retinue of 318 men in his household although other narratives seem to suggest that he has been alone or at most with a few servants;[17] (c) the sudden appearance of the King of Salem, who was hitherto not involved in the war, etc. Were one to isolate vv.18-20 of the narrative, one would achieve a perfect story that flows from the encounter between the king of Sodom and Abram (v.17) to the dialogue that ensued (v.21).[18] This implies that the

---

[14] We have simply adopted the majority translation of the text to indicate that it was Abram that paid tithes to Melchizedek. The Hebrew text indicates in v. 20 that after the blessing by Melchizedek "… he gave him tithes of all." Since the subject of the previous action was Melchizedek, there is at least a rational possibility that it was Melchizedek that paid tithes to Abram. This conclusion would, however, turn our text on its head and render every other application of this text in both the New Testament and rabbinical literature meaningless.

[15] This idea of ritual meal was accepted by N. Airoldi, "La cosiddetta," 195f.

[16] El Elyon is seen in two other places in the Torah (Num 24:16; Deut 32:8). It seems to refer to the highest God in a series of many gods.

[17] N. B. Harmon (ed.), The Interpreter's Bible, Vol. 1 (Genesis), 590.

encounter between Melchizedek and Abram distorts the flow of the narrative.[19] Finally, the total silence between Melchizedek and the king of Sodom is suspicious.

2.3 Abram's Tithe

As already said (→2.1), the offering that Abram made to Melchizedek was in the context of a military expedition that made him rescue his nephew, Lot from the hands of the Eastern kings. As he was returning from the military expedition, Melchizedek, priest of the Most High (El Elyon) offered him bread and wine. This offer by Melchizedek should be seen in the context of refreshment offered to Abram after a long day on the battle field. This is in the context of hospitality which is very important in eastern cultures. This would acquire more currency in many passages of both the OT and the NT. This offer is followed by a biblical unprecedented reciprocation by Abram who offered him a tenth of all the booty he had. The term (maáSër) used to describe the gift of Abram is the adjectival form of the Hebrew word for the number ten.[20] It must then be concluded that what he offered Melchizedek was exactly a tenth of all he had after the battle. These could include livestock, household items, captured agricultural goods, men and women, etc. However, these details were not provided by the biblical narrative.

---

[18] It is surprising that Wenham argues that there are several remarks in Abram's speech to the king of Sodom that are inexplicable without the Melchizedek interruption. Cf. WBC Vol. 1 (Gen 1-15), 306f. We think the only inexplicable remark is that of Wenham. He also tries to make a contrast between the bread offered by Melchizedek and the going out to do battle by the king of Sodom. For him, Melchizedek showed a sign of benevolence while the King of Sodom showed a sign of hostility. But what does one say to the remark of the king of Sodom in v.21?

[19] Scholars who believe that the verses mentioning Melchizedek are to be seen as interpolation include Joseph A. Fitzmyer, "'4QTestimonia' and the New Testament", 64; G. von Rad, Genesis. A Commentary, 175.

[20] Cf. BDB, 798.

But for Melchizedek to qualify to receive tithes from Abram, the nature of his kingship and priestly office over Abram must be established.

2.4 The Kingship of Melchizedek

The personality of the recipient of the gifts (Melchizedek) is also of importance. The fact that critical scholarship has regarded the Melchizedek pericope as a secondary addition makes a concrete depiction of Melchizedek either as a priest or as a king difficult. However, a clearer understanding of his kingship is possible with reference to the notion of divine kingship in the Ancient Near East. A helpful study in this area has been done by Ivan Engnel. He was able to show the divine origin of kings in ancient Egypt[21] and Babylon.[22] Because of this divine origin, the king is "described as the one who has neither father nor mother".[23] The king is not chosen by men but by god long before his birth[24]. His role is felt not only in the daily cults but also at the great festivals.[25] The king's identity with god caused his significant role in the cult in ancient Babylon. For instance, "the king functions as high priest in the cult par excellence".[26] In ancient Hittite culture, the king functions as high priest and appoints the priests.[27] In Babylon, the king was described as a victorious warrior. His soldiers regarded him as a wall, a shield, a fortress and a spring.[28] Righteousness and peace were seen to be the most important characteristics of the king in Ancient Near East.[29] Because of these attributes he was regarded as

---

[21] I. Engnell, Divine Kingship, 4.
[22] I. Engnell, Divine Kingship, 16.
[23] I. Engnell, Divine Kingship, 4.
[24] G. Contenau, Everyday Life, 115.
[25] I. Engnell, Divine Kingship, 5.
[26] I. Engnell, Divine Kingship, 5.
[27] I. Engnell, Divine Kingship, 62.
[28] I. Engnell, Divine Kingship, 12.
[29] S. Langdon, Die Neubabylonischen Königsinschriften, Vorderasiatische Bibliothek 4

the good shepherd by his people, a refuge by the homeless and a father by the widow and orphan.[30] In the Old Testament, too, the king was called "son of God" (Psalms 2:7; 89:27).With these observations, we are in a better place to appreciate the kingly role of Melchizedek.

It is evident that before v.18 of the narrative, no hint is given whatsoever about him. Like a character in a movie, he makes his appearance, performs his role and vanishes just like he came. His name means righteous king or my king is righteous. The significance of names in Ancient Near East shows that righteousness is one of his characteristics. We are told that Melchizedek ruled the city of Salem. The name of Salem that is nowhere else attested in the OT has led some schools of thought to view that it is the shortened form of Shechem, Shilo or Samaria.[31] But it seems that what we have here is a reference to Jerusalem. This is so because the OT itself recognizes that the realm of Melchizedek was Sion (cf. Ps 76:2; 110:2.4). Jerusalem and Sion are found in Ps 51:20; 102:22 and 147:12. Again, 2 Sam 18:18 identifies the Valley of Shavey to be the junction between the two valleys of Kidron and Hinnom.[32] Weinfeld reports that Josephus "in his account about the beginning of Jerusalem (Bellum 6.438ff) relates that Malkizedeq (sic) was the first to officiate as priest in Jerusalem (cf. Gen 14:18, to build the temple there, and to call the city Jerusalem. In other words, Malkizedeq (sic) was the founder of Jerusalem."[33] If this conclusion is true, we are no longer in doubt that Melchizedek reigned over Jerusalem during this time. However, it is difficult to historicize the building of a temple in Jerusalem before the time of Solomon. Identifying

---

(Leipzig: J. C. Hinrichs, 1912), 104. 23f, quoted in I. Engnell, Divine Kingship, 43.

[30] I. Engnell, Divine Kingship, 12.

[31] For these schools of thought see J. A. Emerton's article, "The Site of Salem, the City of Melchizedek (Genesis xiv 18)," in: Studies in the Pentateuch, ed. J. A. Emerton, Supplements to VT XLI (Leiden: Brill, 1990): 45-71.

[32] It could also be the place where Absalom erected a monument for himself (cf. 2 Sm 18:18).

[33] M. Weinfeld, Promise of the Land, 19.

Melchizedek as a king makes the payment made to him by Abram resemble the tithe paid to kings in ancient pagan cultures as donation to the gods who guaranteed victory. But if this is the case, one might then conclude that Melchizedek exercised some overlord power over Abram to necessitate the payment of such a tribute. But if this is the case, a further question arises, namely, why Melchizedek did not get involved in the conflict.

In response to such enquiries, scholars have argued that Melchizedek's territory must have been the smallest of the kingdoms mentioned in the narrative. This could explain his inability to contribute men but his willingness to provide for the material good of the visitors by the offer of bread and wine.[34] On the other extreme are scholars who see Melchizedek as the dominant lord in this region. Representing this line of thought is Wenham who argues that the presentation of bread and wine by Melchizedek was his duty as the dominant ally in the combat.[35] But it is very unlikely to have a dominant ally that played no role in the actual battle.[36] This is unprecedented in the history of oriental kings.[37] Again, if Melchizedek was the king of Jerusalem, as we have argued, then he could not at the same time be the king of the areas around

---

[34] H. H. Rowley, Worship in Ancient Israel, 17-18.

[35] G. J. Wenham, Genesis, WBC 1:316.

[36] But the name Salem could come from shalom, which means peaceful. Cf. R. L. Thomas, New American Standard Hebrew-Aramaic and Greek Dictionaries, 8004. Could this peaceful name have hindered the king of peace from being part of the warfare? But by blessing Abram he showed his support for such expedition.

[37] In Philo's Allegorical Interpretation III. 82 we read the following, "we may therefore call the tyrannical mind the ruler of war, and the kingly mind the guide to peace, that is Salem." In the scrolls of Qumram we find teachings about Melchizedek. In 11QMelchizedek (11Q13), Melchizedek is seen as the one who will carry out the vengeance of God's judgement. Although he is not described as a priest or a king, his priestly status is known from the context and content of his roles. Other fragments that contain references to Melchizedek include 1QApGen ar (1Q20) 22.12-17, 4Q401 fragment 11 and 4Q544 fragments 2-3. For a detailed analysis of these fragments see Dae-Ikang, The Royal Component of Melchizedek in Hebrews, Perichoresis Vol. X. Issue 1 (2012): 95-124.

Mamre where Abram settled (14:13). The distance between Jerusalem and Mamre is about 38 km. From the narrative before us we understand that we are dealing with little kingdoms which may have not extended to such a huge geographical dimension. Thus, it is more logical to conclude that Melchizedek was never an overlord for Abram and his allies. This little note could be of importance in explaining the tithe paid by Abram. If Melchizedek was not a lord over Abram, Abram had no obligation to pay any tributes to him. That means that what Abram gave him was a free donation.

2.5 The Priesthood of Melchizedek

Of equal importance to the question of Abram's gift to Melchizedek is the priestly role of Melchizedek.[38] In the whole context of the payment of tithe in modern times, this role could be said to be more important since the collecting of tithes in the current dispensation is no longer the prerogative of kings but of priests. It would be of interest to identify any king that receives or expects to receive tithes from his subject in this era. On the other hand, priests of various religious sects and denominations see it as a divine mandate to preach and receive tithes. Melchizedek is addressed as the priest of the Most High God (14:18). With him, we encounter the first mention of the priesthood in the OT. But this does not mean that he was the first to perform the priestly function. At the onset of Jewish history, heads of families performed specific priestly duties. Cain and Abel (Gen 4:3f), Noah (Gen 8:20), all offered sacrifices without being instituted as priests. Perhaps this situation led Philo to consider all heads of Jewish families as priests.[39] With regard to the priestly function of Melchizedek, many questions arise similar to the ones posed about his kingship. There are a number of scholars who

---

[38] In Philo's works Melchizedek is described predominantly as a priest. See Allegorical Interpretation III, 79-82 and On Mating with the Preliminary Studies, 99.
[39] Philo, De Vita Mosis II (iii) 224.

identify Melchizedek with Shem, the son of Noah.[40] The main lines of the identification include the similarities between the language of blessing of Genesis 14:19f and Noah's blessing of Shem in Genesis 9:26. Again, between Genesis 9:26 and Genesis 14:18, there is no other place God is identified as the God of anyone apart from Shem. Finally, the rabbis as well as Philo and Josephus identify the God of Melchizedek with the true God. But if Melchizedek is to be identified with Shem, how does one explain the assertion in Hebrews that nothing is known of his ancestry (cf. Heb. 7:3)? However, such an enquiry would take us far away from the object of this present section.

It is good to consider the god Melchizedek was serving. The text simply says that he is a priest of El Elyon. It is widely accepted that the custom of referencing the deity as El was almost a universal usage by the Semitic peoples. The central question, then, is whether the El Elyon which Melchizedek served was the God of Abram. Since the Hebrew religion began with Abraham, accepting that El Elyon was the same God of Abram would be anachronistic. This had led many commentators to accept that El Elyon was only but a local deity.[41] El seems to have some connection with the root ul meaning something like leader, or power or might. In the OT, there are about 238 occurrences of El. As a common name, it designated the divinity of almost the whole of the Semitic world. As a proper name, it was the name of the god of Phoenicia and Canaan. Despite the ancient origin of the name El, Speisser[42] and Gunkel[43] conclude that Israel did not borrow the term from her neigbours. Rather, her neighbours borrowed the term from her. Be that as it may, we are inclined to accepting that since Abram left Ur of the

---

[40] For further research see D. Steinmetz, From Father to Son, 199; F. L. Horton, The Meclchizedek Tradition, 117; M. McNamara, Palestinian Judaism, 210.

[41] See E. A. Speisser, Genesis, 1:104; S. R. Driver, Genesis, 165; H. Gunkel, Genesis, 279-280.

[42] E. A. Speisser, Genesis, 1:104.

[43] H. Gunkel, Genesis, 280.

Chaldeans in order to follow only Yahweh (cf. Gen. 12:1-3), it would be inconceivable that he would accept the blessings of the priest of any other god apart from the priest of Yahweh.[44] It is also in this same sense that the Jewish bible (cf. Ps 110:4) and the New Testament (cf. Heb 5:6.10) understand the priesthood of Melchizedek.

It would also be of interest to investigate into the reality of the priest-king in Jewish culture or her environs. Although this is certainly not attested in the OT, the Jewish priests also performed the functions of kings before the institution of the kingship. Again, some scholars have accepted that it was normal in ancient times for a king to function as a priest for his people.[45] As we have already seen, heads of families even performed the functions of priests in the OT. Abraham himself built altars and offered sacrifices to God (Genesis 13.4 and 22.9). Obviously, if Salem is the same as Jerusalem, by the time of Abram, it was still under the control of the Jebusites, a Canaanite tribe. It was David who conquered Jerusalem in 998 BC and converted it into his political capital. In this case, Melchizedek would be a Canaanite king who performed priestly functions in the name of the God that Abram serves. It might be a puzzle to understand the possibility of a Canaanite king-priest who worships the same God as Abram. But the puzzle might be easily solved when we consider the lack of ancestry of Melchizedek. Considering the importance of genealogies in the OT, are we dealing with a historic figure that has neither father nor mother (Heb 7:3)? This brings us back to the ancillary role of the Melchizedek addition to the Abram saga.

2.6 Summary of Findings

This chapter has exclusively concentrated on the tithe of Abram. In the main, the tithe of Abram resembles the tribute offered in antiquity to the

---

[44] Cf. H. A. Kent, The Epistle to the Hebrews, 124.
[45] See H. Gunkel, Genesis, 280; C. Westermann, Genesis, 2:204f.

temples of the gods who were thought to have assisted the victorious army in the war expedition. Abram's tithe shows that he paid allegiance to the god represented by the priest-king Melchizedek. Apparently, this is the foundational text for the practice of tithing the spoils of war in the extant Jewish corpus. But as we have seen, Abram gave ten percent of the booty to Melchizedek, took a few things for his men of valour, vowed to give the remainder to the king of Sodom and probably went away with nothing. With regard to the later codified law of tithes, this text may not offer much relevance since it has nothing to say about tithing the produce of land which is the exclusive object of the tithing laws which we shall encounter in the next chapter. Selden had argued that the Jewish practice of tithes was neither continuous nor relevant to that of the Christian church. He employed both philological and historical arguments to show that what Abram offered was technically the spoils of war and not tithes.[46] This conclusion is surely in agreement with our findings in this chapter. But even if it is established that the legal stipulations for tithing did not originate from Abram, it does not deny the ancient nature of this law. After all, the law came through Moses and not through Abram.

However, one thing is evident in the Abram saga. We see that the blessing conferred on Abram was not dependent on his payment of tithe. Before he gave Melchizedek a tenth of all he had Melchizedek had already blessed him. If the blessings were dependent on the tithe, Melchizedek would have detained the blessings until the tithe was offered. The only logical conclusion is that the gift by Abram is to be seen as a gift of appreciation. Anything different from this should be regarded as reading into the text.

---

[46] J. Selden, The History of Tithes, 1-3.

CHAPTER THREE
THE CODIFIED MOSAIC LAW AND TITHING

The teaching of tithing in the history of religions is anything but uniform. This is also the case when we turn the searchlight on the Hebrew Scriptures. We have seen hints and projections of this phenomenon in the offerings of Cain and Abel and in the tithing of Abram. But we now intend to focus on the OT passages that legislate on this practice. Concerning the Mosaic legislation on tithing there is profound conflict judging from the fact that the records about this do not agree. For the Encyclopedia Britannica, "the analysis of tithe-legislation in the books ascribed to Moses is a complicated problem."[1] One of the oldest certain allusions to tithe in the Old Testament seems to be Amos 4:4 which mentions tithes paid at Bethel.[2] As already seen, this rite could be as old as the patriarchs Abram (Gen 14:24) and Jacob (cf. Gen 28:22). We shall acquaint ourselves shortly with the codified tithe passages. But before then, an investigation of the covenant stipulation between God and Israel might be helpful.

3.1 The Codified Law

The first codified law of the chosen nation was given in the wilderness. On Sinai, Moses received from God, the book/stone of the covenant (cf. Ex 19-24). This law has to be seen as central to any form of covenant relationship between God and his chosen people. It is because of this centrality that P. R. House makes the following assertions which we quote in affirmation: "There is no way to describe adequately the canonical implications of Exodus 19-24. Everyone from Moses (Deut 5:6-21), to Jeremiah (Jer 7:1-15), to Jesus (Mt 5-7), to Peter (1 Pet 2:9),

---

[1] Encyclopedia Britannica, 1943, Vol.22, s.v "Tithes," especially pages 252-253.

[2] If the Pentateuch was written after the exile as many commentators agree, then the prophet Amos predates the final compilation of the Pentateuch.

53

and every other biblical writer who has anything to say about covenant, morality and relationship to God reflects directly or indirectly on this passage."[3] Obviously, this was not the first covenant between God and humans,[4] but it must be seen as the most profound covenant in the whole of the OT. Although all the OT covenants were made at crucial points in the life of the Jews,[5] the positioning of the Sinai covenant after just before the entrance into the Promised Land gives it more strategic importance.[6] It has been argued that "the history of Israel from this point on is in reality merely a commentary upon the degree of fidelity with which Israel adhered to this Sinai-given vocation."[7] This covenant marks the next stage in the fulfilment of the covenant God made with Abraham.

In this code, almost the whole of the life of a Jew is regulated to the smallest details. Thus, every facet of life is placed under faithful response to God.[8] The numerous usage of the I-Thou language shows that the covenant is to be seen as Yahweh's personal address to his people.[9] In the whole exposition of the covenant relationship between God and the children of Israel, nothing is said about the need to pay a

---

[3] P. R. House, Old Testament Theology, 117.

[4] There were already covenants between God and Noah (Genesis 9:8-17), between God and Abraham (Genesis 15:18; 17). Later, God promised a new Covenant (Jeremiah 31:31-34).

[5] J. H. Walton, Covenant, 51.

[6] For the contextual and theological elements related to Israel's covenants see W. D. Barrick, The Mosaic Covenant, TMSJ 10/2 (Fall 1999), 217.

[7] W. J. Dumbrell, Covenant and Creation, 80.

[8] D. R. Bratcher, Torah as Holiness, n.5. Other important studies about the Mosaic covenant include E. W. Nicholson, God and his People: Covenant and Theology in the Old Testament (Oxford: Clarendon, 1986); R. T. Beckwith, "The Unity and Diversity of God's Covenants," The TynB 38 (1987); F. Brown , S. R. Driver/C. A. Briggs, Hebrew and English Lex icon of the Old Testament (Oxford: Clarendon Press, 1968); G. von Rad, Old Testament Theology (New York: Harper, 1962); M. Weinfield, "Berith—Covenant vs. Obligation," TDOT, 2:255-56.

[9] Cf. J M. Sprinkle, Law and Narrative in Exodus 19-24, JETS 47/2 (June 2004) 235-252, here 236f.

tenth of one's income. One is bound to question why the issue of tithing is not included in this divine code.[10] Considering the importance of the covenant in the life of the Jews, this absence is very disturbing. But this is just the beginning.

Even when Moses needed money to finance the new nation under his care, he appealed to his people for freewill donations. The result was that "men and women, as many as were willing hearted, brought bracelets, and earrings, and rings, and tablets, all jewels of gold and ... the children of Israel brought a willing offering unto the Lord ... They brought yet unto him [Moses] free offerings every morning ... the stuff they had was sufficient for all the work to make it, and too much" (Ex 35:22.29; 36:37). The words that should be underlined in this citation are "willing offering." Indeed, it was God who expressly commanded Moses to make the appeal of free offering to the people (Ex 25:1-8) for the building of a sanctuary for Yahweh. Many verses in this section (35:21.22.26.29) emphasize the free nature of these offerings. We are not told whether the gifts presented by the Israelites had anything to do with the spoils they collected from Egypt. If that is the case, then this corresponds to the ancient practice of presenting the spoils of war to the god of the victorious nation. The sufficiency of the offering brought by the Israelites was so that the people had to be restrained from bringing more gifts. This is a subtle biblical remark that may not carry much weight. But is it possible to think of any Christian gathering where the leaders for once tell the members to stop contributing?

Meanwhile, it seems that a year passed in the desert before Moses realized the importance of tithes. We shall see this in the book of Leviticus. Before this time, various forms of sacrifices and rituals were prominent but the practice of tithing was notable through its absence. There must be new developments that necessitated this realization.

---

[10] However, Leviticus 27:30-34 remarks that tithe is part of the law given to Moses on Mt Sinai. Is this a priestly addition?

We begin with the sin of the golden calf (Ex 32).[11] After the abomination of Aaron's[12] erection of the calf and the revelry of the Israelites, the Levites who rallied round Moses and meted out divine vengeance to fellow Israelites (Ex 32:26-28) became the official priests in the Mosaic religion.[13] During the distribution of land among the twelve tribes of Israel, the Levites (the priests included) received no inheritable land either from Moses or from Joshua. Instead, they are to receive portions of land from the other tribes as a form of gift. This lack of inheritance to the Levites as well as the command to allot them land

----

[11] There is no intention to make elaborate analysis of the golden calf episode here. Lack of scholarly consensus on this episode is shown by the fact that different scholars have assigned it to different sources. J. I. Durham, Exodus, WBC, vol. 3 (Waco, TX, 1987), 417, 427-428, 435, presents an array of scholarly views on this episode. See also B. S. Childs, The Book of Exodus, 559. He views that the narrative has a basic J source with some expansions; I. Lewy, "The Story of the Golden Calf Reanalysed," VT 9 (1959): 318, sees a Yahwist narrative groundwork and four editors, a Yahwist, a northern prophetic Elohist, a southern priestly Elohist, and a Deuteronomist. R. E. Friedman, in Who Wrote the Bible?, 70, sees the episode as being originally an E narrative.

[12] The survival of Exodus 32 in the Pentateuch supposed to have been edited by the Priests has led to much scholarly discussion. For a survey of critical approaches to the story of the golden calf, see K. Schmid, "Israel am Sinai," 9-40; J. J., Watts, "Aaron and the Golden Calf," JBL 130, no. 3 (2011): 417-430. However, the Aaronide hand can be felt in the OT with regard to the fact that many OT passages narrate this story without mention of Aaron. Deuteronomy 33:8-11 could be referring to the golden calf story to celebrate the Levites' ordination, but makes no mention of Aaron. Psalm 106:19-23 omits Aaron entirely from its summary of the story. This is very important because few verses earlier it calls Aaron "holy to YHWH" while recalling the rebellion of Dathan and Abiram (v.16). Although Nehemiah 9:18 quotes the words "these are your gods" it omits Aaron in its allusion to the golden calf in a longer historical summary. Later Jewish historians also showed much respect to Aaron. While Philo (Moses 2.159-73) omitted the mention of Aaron in his retelling of the story, Josephus omits the story entirely even as he mentioned the fear of the Israelites during Moses' long absence (Ant. 3.95-101).

[13] For arguments that the narrative which echoes the acclamation of Jeroboam I (I Kgs 12:28) equals polemic against the Aaronite priests of the northern kingdom see W. M. L. de Wette, Einleitung, 247; J. Wellhausen, Hexateuch, 91-92. Of course these arguments are based on the conclusion that the whole of Exodus 32 is a post-exilic writing.

from the other tribes is contained in many portions of the Jewish scriptures (cf. Num 35:2-4; Josh 20:21, I Chron 6:48-81; II Chron 31:15-19, and Neh 10:37). The above passages show that this state of affairs was current during the first and second Temple periods. Their having some form of land means that the priests and Levites did not spend their whole time ministering in the Temple since they had some arable land on which to cultivate. History also shows that the priests took turns in ministering in the Temple according to their clans. The fact that they were scattered in all the tribes makes a permanent service in the Temple of Jerusalem geographically impossible. This is a situation that can never be replicated in the life of any living religion of our era. The sustenance of the Levites depended largely on the tithes provided by the remaining eleven tribes. This is the origin of the Mosaic tithe.

3.2 The Composite Nature of the Pentateuch

As said above, the command to the people of Israel to tithe was initiated in the book of Leviticus. Before delving into the Mosaic legislation, it would serve a useful purpose to direct the mind of the reader to the four sources from which the Torah is composed. According to the seminal work of J. Wellhausen,[14] the Torah is the product of several stages of the gathering of diverse theological documents, writing and rewriting them until what we have today emerged. According to Wellhausen's formulation we have four sources: the Yahwist source (J): written c. 950 BCE in the southern Kingdom of Judah; the Elohist source (E): written c. 850 BCE in the northern Kingdom of Israel; the Deuteronomist (D): written c. 600 BCE in Jerusalem during a period of religious reform; the Priestly source (P): written c. 500 BCE by Kohanim (Jewish priests) in exile in Babylon. For Wellhausen, these four sources were finally edited by the priestly school into the Pentateuch after the exile. This is the

---

[14] J. Wellhausen, Prolegomenon zur Geschichte Israels, 1878. However, the first person to note the use of different sources in the Mosaic books was Jean Astruc.

classical four-source theory or the documentary hypothesis. This is a complex hypothesis that has been summarized for the purpose of our enquiry. Although it is only a hypothesis and as such subject to the limitations of any other hypotheses, it explains some of the apparent contradictions we find in the OT narrative as the product of the compilation of writings from different sources.

Although this is not the place to review scholarly opinion on the implication and extent of this division of the Torah into a composite unit,[15] a few elaborations can be made about it with reference to its implication for the theology of tithe. First, the earlier sources of the Torah (the J and E sources), seem to be silent or at least reticent on the issue of tithing. We get most of our information about tithing from the priestly and Deuteronomist traditions. The priestly source includes most of Leviticus (Levites). The Deuteronomist includes most of Deuteronomy. This makes us to understand who is talking when we read the words: "All tithes from the land, whether the seed from the ground or the fruit from the tree, are the Lord's; they are holy to the Lord" (Lev. 27:30). These terse words have received a lot of comments and interpretations in the history of biblical research. This is important since it also received several reformulations in the Pentateuch itself. In many other parts of the Pentateuch, the object and aim of the tithe are made explicit. We shall make these passages as clear as possible. We shall begin with the kinds of tithe evident in the Torah.

---

[15] For critiques of this hypothesis see D. A. Garrett's Rethinking Genesis (Grand Rapids, 1991); R. Rendtorff, The Problem of the Process of Transmission in the Pentateuch, trans. by John Scullion, JSOT Sup 89 (Sheffield, 1990); D. A. Garrett, "The Documentary Hypothesis," The Bible and Spade 6 (1993). For Garrettt, "the documentary hypothesis must be abandoned." D. A. Garrett, "The Documentary Hypothesis," 49.

3.3 Israel's Three Tithes

A most important area of conflict in the tithe-legislation of the Old Testament is the number or types of tithes to be offered by the Jewish people. Here, scholars fail to agree. While some argue for the existence of three different kinds of types, others accept only two types. It could be argued that Josephus mentions three tithes. He writes: "Let there be taken out of your fruits a tenth, besides that which you have allotted to give to the priests and Levites. This you may indeed sell in the country, but it is to be used in those feasts and sacrifices that are to be celebrated in the holy city; for it is fit that you should enjoy those fruits of the earth which God gives you to possess, so as may be to the honor of the donor."[16] We surely have a record of two different tithes here. The first is the one giving to the priests and the Levites while the second is the one to be sold in the city and used for sacrificial meals. The third type is the one to be offered for the poor in the land. Again Josephus writes: "Beside those two tithes which I have already said you are to pay every year, the one for the Levites, the other for the festivals, you are to bring every third year a tithe to be distributed to those that want; to women also that are widows, and to children that are orphans."[17] We shall now devote some time to looking at these different tithes.

3.3.1 The First Tithe (ma'aser rishon)

We are now in a position to examine more fully the distinctions in the Mosaic tithes. Some portions of the Hebrew bible seem to support the view of Josephus to the existence of three different tithes. The first tithe is seen in Leviticus 27:30-33:

> "And all the tithe of the land, whether of the seed of the land, or
> of the fruit of the tree, is the Lords: it is holy unto the Lord. And
> if a man will redeem part of his tithe, he shall add unto it a fifth

---

[16] Josephus, Antiquities, Ch. IV, Bk VIII, 8.
[17] Josephus, Antiquities, bk. 4.

part thereof. And concerning the tithe of the herd, or of the flock, even of whatsoever passes under the rod, the tenth shall be holy unto the Lord. He shall not search whether it be good or bad, neither shall he change it: and if he change it at all, then both it and that for which it is changed shall be holy; it shall not be redeemed."

This passage probably from the priestly source has at least four implications: (a) That a tenth of the produce of the land, whether of seed or fruit, was claimed by God, and was to be regarded as holy (or set apart) for Him by Israel; (b) That if the one making the offering wished to retain this tenth of seed or fruit, he might do so by paying its value, and adding thereto one-fifth; (c) That every tenth calf and lamb also (that is, increase of the herd or flock) was to be set apart for the Lord; (d) There is no provision for the redemption of the tithe from the flock. The main aim of this tithe is to provide for the needs of the Levites. This is made explicit in Numbers 18:21. That is the explanation of the phrase "holy unto the Lord." This is simply logical since it serves as the means of ensuring the survival of the Levites. This is why this tithe can be called the Lord's or the Levite's tithe. In rabbinic literature, it is known as the first tithe.[18]

One can also point out some other basic marks of this tithe. We observe that from this tithing only produce of land, or increase of herd or flock, is expected. Nothing is said of monetary offering. It also seems that the offerer has no voice in its disposal. It is his duty to offer the tithe and not worry about its use. More so, though it was called a heave offering, the offerer did not receive any of it back again. Finally, there is no mention of offering the tithe for the maintenance of the priests. Those in view as recipients of the tithes are the Levites who ministered in the

---

[18] Cf. L. H. Schiffman, The Provo International Conference on the Dead Sea Scrolls, Vol. XXX, 488.

Temple in Jerusalem. The above points are concretized in the text of Deuteronomy 14:27-29 which mandates the Israelites not to forsake the Levites within their towns since they have no allotment or inheritance.

There is another legislation in the Jewish Scriptures that concerns this first tithe. This legislation is contained in Numbers 18:21:32. The text makes it explicit that all the tithes paid to the Levites belong to them in exchange for the work they do in the house of God (Num 18:21.24.31). The implication is that tithes were the wages of the Levites for their work. Thus, they were receiving wages commensurate with their work in protecting the sanctuary and rendering other cultic services. By paying their tithe, the people fulfil their covenantal obligations and at the same time pay the Levites for their sacred functions.[19] Nonetheless, the Levites are to make an offering to the priests from the tithe paid to them (Num 18:26.28). This is where the Levites fulfil their covenantal obligations. This is one of the many instances where economics is mixed with religion in Judaism. During the time of the second Temple, this tithe was also renewed as recorded in Nehemiah 13:5.12. Here, the list of the products to be tithed included corn, new wine and oil.

On the other hand McConvile argues that;

Nehemiah knew the legislation of Deuteronomy as well as of Numbers and Leviticus, yet represented only a single tithe. Here is what ought to be a final answer to the old Jewish solution. The idea of multiple tithes, having ancient Jewish tradition behind it, should not be lightly dismissed. But it fails because it is not the most ancient Jewish interpretation. That honour belongs to the book of Nehemiah, whose author knew all the relevant laws but only one tithe.[20]

---

[19] J. Milgrom, Leviticus 23-27: A New Translation, 2433.
[20] J. G. McConville, Law and Theology in Deuteronomy, 75.

The argument of McConville is that the practice during the second Temple period was only the offering of one tithe based on the text of Nehemiah 13. What he forgets is that Nehemiah's interest was on the tithe paid to the Levites and not on other types of tithes.[21] We shall later see the historical facts that led Nehemiah to insist on the payment of the first tithe.

3.3.2 The Second Tithe (ma'aser shen)

The second tithe can be gleaned from a passage in Deuteronomy. The relevant section is from Deuteronomy 14:22-27:

> "Be sure to set aside a tenth of all that your fields produce each year. Eat the tithe of your grain, new wine and olive oil, and the firstborn of your herds and flocks in the presence of the Lord your God at the place he will choose as a dwelling for his Name, so that you may learn to revere the Lord your God always. But if that place is too distant and you have been blessed by the Lord your God and cannot carry your tithe (because the place where the Lord will choose to put his Name is so far away), then exchange your tithe for silver, and take the silver with you and go to the place the Lord your God will choose. Use the silver to buy whatever you like: cattle, sheep, wine or other fermented drink, or anything you wish. Then you and your household shall eat there in the presence of the Lord your God and rejoice. And do not neglect the Levites living in your towns, for they have no allotment or inheritance of their own."

This passage can be made clearer by elucidating the implications. They include the following: (a) That it consisted of the yearly increase of the land. This tithe specifically mentions grain, wine and oil; (b) That it was

---

[21] See also L. H. Schiffman, "Priestly and Levitical Gifts," in: The Provo International Conference, 488.

to be eaten by the offerer, his household, and the Levite; (c) The object of this was that Israel might always fear Yahweh; (d) That it might be converted at home into money, to be expended at the capital for sacrifices and feasting; (e) The tithe-payer was to eat and rejoice before God. Unlike the first tithe whose aim is to provide for the needs of the Levites, this second tithe has more of a communal character. This explains why it is also called the festival tithe.

Some Temple scrolls (cf. 11 QT43:4-10) join the obligation to offer the second tithe to the celebration of the feast of the first fruits. The possibility of exchanging this tithe for money may be to enable the offerer to carry the proceeds to Jerusalem for the communal celebration.[22] This is elucidated in Deuteronomy 12:6-7. This idea of sacrificial meal offered to the deity seems to be a universal motif that forms the background of sacrifices in many religions.[23] Evidence shows that in some cases, the sacrifice is burnt entirely to the deity, but in most cases, the offerers share in the sacrificial meal. This last case seems to be what applied in the Jewish festival tithe. If one is to compare the first and second types of tithes, one notices that while the tithe giver has no voice in terms of the disposition of the first tithe he can determine how the second tithe is to be disposed of. Again, while the tithe giver does not receive any portion of the first tithe, the second tithe allows him to receive some portion of the tithe. This tithe is also attested in the rabbinic teachings.[24]

3.3.3 The Third Tithe (ma'aser 'ani)

We now come to the third tithe. This is done every three years. Its aim is to take care of the Levite, the stranger, the motherless and the widow.

---

[22] Cf. L. H. Schiffman, "Priestly and Levitical Gifts," The Provo International Conference, Vol. 30, 489.

[23] Cf. W. R. Smith (ed.), Encyclopaedia Britannica (9th ed.), s.v "Sacrifice," Vol. 21, 132.

[24] Cf. L. H. Schiffman, The Courtyards of the House of the Lord, 548-550.

The offerer of this tithe receives divine blessings from God. Our proof-text is Deuteronomy 14:28-29:

> "At the end of every three years, bring all the tithes of that year's produce and store it in your towns, so that the Levites (who have no allotment or inheritance of their own) and the foreigners, the fatherless and the widows who live in your towns may come and eat and be satisfied, and so that the Lord your God may bless you in all the work of your hands."

The tithe in view here could be called the tithe of the poor, a form of charity.[25] In the third and sixth year, the tithe goes to the poor. In the seventh year, the land lies fallow and there is no planting and no harvesting (cf. Ex 23:10f; Lev 25:2-7) and thus no tithe. It is instructive that the Levite is numbered among the poor of the land, together with the foreigners, the fatherless and the widow. This is a minor fact that could have a major impact in present day application of the tithe. It appears that those who have more are the ones that pay this tithe for the benefit of the less privileged. Meanwhile, the offering of this tithe is to be accompanied by prayer by the one who has paid the tithe. The book of Deuteronomy gives a model for such a prayer: "I have removed from my house the sacred portion and have given it to the Levite, the alien, the fatherless and the widow, according to all you commanded. I have not transgressed nor forgotten any of your commandments…Look down from heaven…and bless your people Israel and the land you have given us…" (Deut. 26:13-15). We thus have three types of tithes in the Pentateuch.

The book of Tobit is also in support of these three distinctions. While informing his readers about the falling away from the dictates of God by

---

[25] For Maimonides, "in as much as the man and his household would not be likely to consume the whole of the tithe, he would be compelled to give part away in charity." Quoted in J. R. Lundblom, Deuteronomy: A Commentary, 484.

his people, Tobit asserts that he is the only one who has followed the commands of God. "I alone went often to Jerusalem at the feasts, as it hath been ordained unto all Israel by an everlasting decree, having the first fruits and the tenths of mine increase, and that which was first shorn; and I gave them at the altar to the priests, the sons of Aaron. The tenth part of all mine increase I gave to the sons of Levi, who ministered at Jerusalem: and the second tenth apart I sold away, and went; and spent it each year at Jerusalem: and the third I gave unto them for whom it was meet, as Deborah my father's mother had commanded me" (Tobit 1:6-8). What Tobit added here is that he paid the tithes to the priests. If this means that he gave the tithe for the consumption of the priest, then he presents us with a situation that is nowhere attested in the OT.[26] These witnesses of a third tithe are corroborated by ancient exegetes. Jerome, who lived in Palestine, says that one tithe was given to the Levites from which they gave a part to the priests, a second tithe was a festive one while the third was given to the poor.[27] The implication of the above distinction is that two tithes were to be taken every year except in the seventh year. In the first, second, fourth and fifth years, the first and second tithes were to be taken. In the third and sixth years, the first and third tithes were to be taken.

Despite these distinctions, some scholars argue that what we have identified as a third tithe is only but a triennial substitution for the second tithe. This means that in the third year and in the sixth year, the people of Israel would not take the second tithe to the house of God. Rather, they would dispose of it among the poor in their midst. For

---

[26] Curiously, J. R. Rundblom argues that Lev 27:30-33 directs the tithes for the use of the priests. See his Deuteronomy: A Commentary, 484. His supposition is difficult to defend.

[27] Jerome, Commentary on Ezekiel 45:1, 565. Quoted in J. McClintock/J. Strong, The Cyclopedia of Biblical, Theological, and Ecclesiastical Literature, Vol. X, 434. See also Chrysostom who saw three tithes in Judaism. For he asks and answers: "What, then, did they (the Jews) give? A tenth of all their possessions, and another tenth, and after this a third (tenth)," etc. (Homily 64 on Matthew 20:27).

instance, Maimonides, a respected rabbi of the 12th century denies the existence of a third tithe. In his own words, "on the third and sixth years from the sabbatical year, after they have separated the first tithe, they separate from what remains another tithe, and give it to the poor, and it is called the poor's tithe; and not on those two years is the second tithe, but the poor's tithe."[28] The reader has the mandate to judge between the statements of Tobit, written in the third century, coupled with the testimony of Jerome, who lived in Palestine four years later and the comments of Maimonides who flourished in Spain in the twelfth century when the Jews were already dispersed and who may not have experienced the payment of tithes. The Jewish encyclopedia records that Jewish sources discuss three kinds of tithes but no more than two were accessed in a single year.[29] Selden and Michaelis also argue in the same direction, saying that a third tithe should be an excessive demand upon the income of a man who had already expended two-tenths of his increase.[30] Peake likewise says: "It may be urged that it is not probable that a double tribute should be exacted from the crops." And again: "Nor is it probable that a tax of nearly one-fifth of the whole produce should be imposed on the farmers."[31] From a common sense point of view, this would be an exaction on the poor people whose subsistence depended mainly or exclusively from the produce of the land. The New Unger's bible dictionary summarizes that of these opinions that which maintains three different and complete tithing seems improbable.[32] According to Harper's bible dictionary, "discrepancies between regulations concerning tithing ...resulted to the Mishna's adopting two tithes. The first was for the Levites and the second was to be eaten by the people."[33]

---

[28] Maimonides, Hilchot Mattanot Anayim, c. 6, sect. 4; M. F. Unger, The New Unger's Bible Dictionary, s.v. "Tithe", 1291.
[29] The Jewish Encyclopedia, Vol. 12, s.v "Tithe", 151.
[30] J. McClintock/J. Strong Encyclopaedia, Vol. X, 434.
[31] J. Hastings Dictionary of the Bible, Vol. I, 780.
[32] Cf. S. M. Collins, Biblical Teachings, 2.

This implies that the tithe for the poor has been eliminated. But it has to be noted that the Mishna was created around AD 200. This means that it is a compilation of post-biblical law. This could mean that the concept of only two tithes did not originate in the bible. As already argued, the Jewish bible has given us three tithes.

3.4 Distinction Between Priest and Levite

We have reached a stage in our research where it has become necessary to make a distinction between the priests and the Levites of the OT. It is our feeling that the whole discussion about the payment of tithes for the sustenance of the Levites may not be meaningful to the reader without a clear description of who a Levite was in the Jewish religion and how he differed from the priest.[34] Levi was one of the children of Jacob. In fact, he was the third son of Jacob born to him by Lea (Gen 35:23). Although Levi was notorious for his fiery temperament (cf. Gen 34, 49, Ex 32 and Deut 33), he was still chosen to be set apart for a special mission.[35] Following the Golden Calf incident (cf. Ex 32:26-29), this tribe was set apart for special service to the God of Israel. Theologically speaking, this incident turned the curse given to them by their father that they would be scattered throughout Israel (cf. Gen 49:5-7)[36] into a blessing.[37] Their special status was accentuated by divine decree in Numbers 1-4.

---

[33] Cf. S. M. Collins, Biblical Teachings, 3.

[34] Obviously, the biblical accounts represent the end-product of the reflections of the Hebrew people and might not be an exact account of history. But we have presented the following survey based on the end reconstruction of the Jewish bible. Good books and articles are available on the historical development of the priesthood in Ancient Israel. See for example E. Nielsen, "The Levites in Ancient Israel," in: Law, History and Tradition: Selected Essays by Eduard Nielsen, Copenhagen, 1983, 71-81; M. D. Rehm, "Levites and Priests," in ABD 4:297-310; A. Cody, A History of Old Testament Priesthood, Rome, 1969; Antonius H. J. Gunneweg, Leviten und Priester, Göttingen, 1965.

[35] The violent origin of the Levites has been researched by J. S. Baden, "The Violent Origins of the Levites: Text and Tradition," in Levites and Priests in Biblical History and Tradition, Mark Leuchter and J. M. Huton (ed) (SBL 9 2011), 103-106.

Although all the priests were from the tribe of Levi (hence the Levitical priesthood), not all Levites were priests. The tribe of Levi had three clans: Gershon, Kohath, and Merari. Before the building of the Temple, these clans already had some cultic functions. The Tabernacle was instituted on Mt. Sinai in 1446 BC. It was during this period that special functions were allotted to each of the three lines of Levites. Some of the duties of the Gershonites included moving tabernacle covers, curtains, screens and cords with ox carts (cf. Num 4:24-26; 7:7f).[38] The Gershonites were to camp behind the tabernacle westward (Num 3:23). The Merarites camped on the north side of the tabernacle (Num 3:33-37). Merarite duties involved moving tabernacle poles, boards, sockets, pillars and bars individually by hand (Num 3:36f; 4:29-33). The duties of the sons of Kohath included moving the Ark and holy furniture with poles (Num 4:4-12; 7:7-9). The Kohathites camped on the south side of the tabernacle (Num 3:29). It is from this clan that Aaron descended. Already in the desert, the special position of the Levites was recognized. The book of Deuteronomy writes: "Now if a Levite comes from any of your towns throughout Israel where he resides, and comes whenever he desires to the place which the Lord chooses, then he shall serve in the name of the Lord his God, like all his fellow Levites who stand there before the Lord" (Deut 18:6-7). The above injunction is understandable from the point of lack of inheritance for the descendants of Levi. The systematic allocation of land conquered from the Canaanites to the tribes of Israel started in numbers 32:33 by Moses and

---

[36] For the age and nature of this poem see F. M. Cross/D. N. Freedman, Studies in Ancient Yahwist Poetry (1950), New Edition, Biblical Resource Series, Grand Rapids, 1997, 46-47.

[37] This could explain the preservation of the story of the golden calf. In this light it becomes the legitimization of the ordination of the Levites. As J. J. Watt puts it "the golden calf story fills this lacuna with a positive explanation for why the Levites gained their status as the guardians of the sanctuary." See his "Aaron and the Golden Calf in the Rhetoric of the Pentateuch," JBL 130, no. 3 (2011), 426.

[38] See also Num. 3:25f; 4:24-26.

was concluded in Joshua 19:51. The only landed property given to the Levites was only towns to live in, with pasturelands for their flocks and herds (cf. Josh 14:4). Since their main task it so function in the tabernacle, there must be a system that provides for their upkeep. This is what the codified Mosaic tithe aimed at fulfilling. This is to be understood by the statement that the priestly service of the Lord is their inheritance (Josh 18:7).

In as much as the above situation affects the Levites and the priests, the priests seem to enjoy some privileged status above the Levite. With reference to liturgical responsibility, it was only Aaron and his descendants that were allowed to offer incense or animal sacrifice in the Tabernacle. The revolt of the other clans of Levi against this exclusive status of the Aaronides ended in a fiasco of tremendous proportion (cf. Num 16:39f). We could then conclude that the priests were the ones that performed the main task of burning of incense and presenting the offerings in the Temple while the Levites were the ones involved in other cultic responsibilities. The division of labour is such that those not from Aaron's direct family cannot become High Priests (Ex 28:2), the Levites cannot become priests (Num 16-17) and members of other tribes cannot become Levites (Num 8:14).[39] However, guarding the sanctuary seems to be a collective responsibility of both priests and Levites, with the Levites guarding from outside.

During the first Temple period,[40] some of the duties of the Levites included the following: 24,000 Temple Workers (I Chron 23:4); 6,000 civil and religious judges and officers (I Chron 23:4; 26:29-31); 4,000 civil and religious guards (I Chron 23:5); 4,000 singers (I Chron 23:5); 4,600 earlier served as soldiers (1 Chron. 12:23, 26) (1 Chron 27:5).[41]

---

[39] P. P. Jenson, Graded Holiness, 117.

[40] The relationship between the priests and Levites in Judaism in the first Temple period has been studied by Joachim Schaper, Priester und Leviten im achämenidischen Juda: Studien zur Kult- und Socialgeschichte Israels in persischer Zeit (FAT 31; Tübingen, 2000.

These were the tasks of the 38,000 tithe-receiving Levites during the time of King David. The roles played by the Levites show that they were skilled in many crafts and arts. It also seems they were political leaders as well as other OT passages attest. R. E. Kelly has argued that "there were 6,000 Levites who served as governmental judges and treasurers in the Levitical cities: 1,700 judged and collected revenue in one region of the country, 2,700 in another region, and (evidently) 1,600 in a third region."[42] This means the tithes of the Israelites were used for the upkeep of the king's officials who doubled as Levites during this time. This was because the Jerusalem Temple could be called a royal Temple at this time.

Although it is not the main point of our discussion, any attempt to schematize the Jewish priesthood cannot fail to say a word or two about the holiness code of the priestly class.[43] Although Israel is a holy nation, there was to be a clear distinction between the holiness of the priests on the one and that of the Levites and the people on the other hand.[44] This was why the priests could perform cultic activities on behalf of the people who stood at a distance. The ordination of Aaron and his sons with all the details (Ex 28-29/Lev 8-9) show the holiness prescriptions clearly. One has the impression that the holiness of the priesthood mirrors exactly the holiness of the tabernacle. Maybe this aspect of the Levitical priesthood needs to be emphasized more than anything else.

---

[41] Cf. R. E. Kelly, Should the Church Teach Tithing? 69f.

[42] R. E. Kelly, Should the Church Teach Tithing? 70.

[43] Uncountable studies have been devoted to the so-called holiness code of Lev 17-26. Some of the ones in English include: L. E. Elliot-Binns, "Some Problems of the Holiness Code," ZAW 65 (1955), 26-40; I. Knohl, "The Priestly Torah Versus the Holiness School: Sabbath and the Festivals," HUCA 58 (1987), 65-117; I. Knohl, "The Law of Sin-Offering of the Holiness School," Tarbiz 59 (1989-90), 1-9; J. Joosten, People and Land in the Holiness Code: An Exegetical Study of Ideational Framework of the Law in Leviticus 17-26, Leiden, 1966; R. E. Gane and A. T. Cohen (ed), Current Issues in Priestly and Related Literature: The Legacy of Jacob Milgrom and Beyond, 2015.

[44] Cf. P. P., Jenson, Graded Holiness, 119.

If we are allowed to move from the Jewish religion to any other religion, we could then assert that if there is still any religion that employs the services of priests, then the Levites should be those that help the priests in carrying out their priestly functions. This would then include the choristers, lectors, altar servers, church warden, etc. It was this set of people that the OT tithes were meant for. This is where the whole principle of OT tithing should be looked into with another lens.

3.5 Priestly Offerings and Levitical Tithes

Since we have dwelt much on the Levitical tithes, it would serve some useful purpose to identify the offerings exacted from the people for the maintenance of the priestly class. It is not to be presumed that God would ensure that the Levites are sustained through the institution of the tithe while leaving the sons of Aaron destitute. As said above, it was the exclusive function of the priests to offer incense and animal sacrifice in the tabernacle and in the Temple. As we shall come to see, apart from the burnt offering or holocaust, in which the whole animal is offered to God, the priest gets a share of every sacrificial victim. Consequently, the Torah is clear on the portion of the offering that belongs to Aaron and his descendants. The relevant section is Num. 18:8-9.11-14. It says:

> I myself have put you in charge of the offerings presented to me; all the holy offerings the Israelites give me I give to you and your sons as your portion, your perpetual share. You are to have the part of the most holy offerings that is kept from the fire. From all the gifts they bring me as most holy offerings, whether grain or sin or guilt offerings, that part belongs to you and your sons... This also is yours: whatever is set aside from the gifts of all the wave offerings of the Israelites. I give this to you and your sons and daughters as your perpetual share. Everyone in your household who is ceremonially clean may eat it. I give you all the finest olive oil and all the finest new wine and grain they give the

Lord as the first fruits of their harvest. All the land's first fruits that they bring to the Lord will be yours. Everyone in your household who is ceremonially clean may eat it. Everything in Israel that is devoted to the Lord is yours.

By way of clarity, the priestly portions can be identified[45] as the tenufah and terumah (Lev 7:29-36); firstlings and first fruits (Ex 13:11-15; Lev 2:14-16; Num 18:12-18; Deut 18:4; 26:1-11); and gifts including vows and dedications (Lev 27). The firstling of man was to be redeemed by the payment of five shekels.[46] The firstling of a cow, goat or sheep might not be redeemed but was to be brought to the altar and the flesh becomes the property of the priest after it has been offered to God (cf. Deut 18:16-17). With all probability there was no specified quantity of the first fruits to be offered. For Maimonides, the virtuous man offered one of forty, a middling brought one of fifty while a covetous man offered one of sixty.[47] There also other numerous offerings or sacrifices enjoined on the Jews in the books of the Torah. Most of the victims of these sacrifices ended in the household of the priests. We shall see these in the next chapter. One is then justified in questioning the need for a tithe to be paid by the Levites to the priests since God had already ensured the source of livelihood for the sons of Aaron. It could be said with some level of informed deduction that the first or Levitical tithe should be for the upkeep of the sons of Levi (the Kohathites excluded). From this ten percent, the Levites are to pay a tithe to the priests who are not to pay any tithes at all. This is one way the tithe paid by the Levites

---

[45] These items have been summarized by L. L. Grabbe, Judaic Religion, 137. Nonetheless, Grabbe includes the tithes on all agricultural products as the main source of income for the priests. He seems to have neglected the distinction between priest and Levite in Judaism despite the fact that he acknowledged the tithe paid to the Levites on the same page of his book.
[46] Cf. H. Lansdell, Sacred Tenth, 1:71.
[47] Cf. H. Lansdell, Sacred Tenth, 1:70.

to the priests could make any sense. Converting this argument into a contemporary language makes it easier to understand. If a Jew receives 1000 dollars as his income from the resources of the land, he makes a payment of 100 dollars to the Levite. The Levite, who does the menial jobs in the house of God then pays 10 dollars to the priest who does the more detailed cultic functions. This means that the priests receives one percent of the tithes of the people. With the understanding that there are more Jews than Levites, what accrues to the priest from the tithes of the people would be nothing in comparison to what the Levite receives. This is then balanced by the sacrificial items that are the exclusive portion of the priests. This system must have been fair enough for both priests and Levites.

3.6 The Tithes in Rabbinical Literature

Before drawing the curtain on this chapter, a few words could be said about rabbinical legislation on biblical tithing. It is to be accepted that the rabbis do not serve as authoritative interpreters of the Jewish Scriptures for Christians. Therefore, their conclusions must not be seen as normative for Christians. Again, different rabbinical schools do not agree on different passages in their bible. Yet, it might serve some cognitive purpose to explore some of their teachings with regard to the content and merit of tithing. The reason is simple: it must be accepted that the rabbis are closer to the Jewish tradition than Christian theologians. It should also be noted that the teachings of the rabbis represent, in the main, the actual practice of tithing when Christianity matured.

According to the rabbis, there are rules to determine which goods are to be tithed. It must be eatable, the property of an individual, and the product of the soil. We first make reference to the first division of the Mishna which deals with seeds or matters relating to agriculture. In the seventh book,[48] we read the following words:

"this general rule has been handed down about the tithe: whatever serves for food, is worth keeping, and grows out of the ground, is subject to tithe: and another rule handed down is, that whatever is eatable at the beginning, as well as when fully grown, although customarily kept till it is mature, is subject to tithes, be it small or grown large. But when, in its early stages it is not an ordinary article of food, but becomes so later, it is not subject to tithe until fit to be eaten."[49]

The above citation shows that the Jewish practice during the time between the two testaments focused on the tithing of agricultural products. Not only was tithing restricted to agricultural products, the very products to be offered as tithes have to be scrutinized. For instance, figs when they begin to ripen, grapes when transparent and mulberries when they turn red a subject to tithe.[50] Therefore, when one eats untithed fruit in an immature state, he is not guilty of having transgressed the Law. But if the fruit is already ripe and not tithed, the eater incurs the wrath of divine transgression.

The earlier rabbis applied the law of tithing to Egypt and to the lands of Ammon and Moab (Yad. iv. 3); and the scribes seem to have instituted tithes in Syria.[51] The sources do not explain why tithes have to be locally limited but a critical mind reveals that this could be because the payment of tithe is connected to the Temple which obviously is non-existent in alien soil. However, some rabbis think that the third tithe, that is, the tithe to the poor gave rise to the tithing of ones earnings. For some rabbis, this is an obligation imposed by Mosaic Law. For others, on the other hand, tithing ones earnings is imply a custom and is not obligatory either under the Mosaic or under the rabbinical law.[52]

---

[48] Ch. I Sect I.
[49] Quoted in H. Lansdell, Sacred Tenth, 1:120.
[50] Cf. H. Lansdell, Sacred Tenth, 1:121.
[51] Cf. J. Jacobs/M. Seligsohn/W. Bacher, Jewish Encyclopedia, s.v. "Tithe."
[52] Cf. J. acobs/M. Seligsohn/W. Bacher, Jewish Encyclopedia, s.v. "Tithe."

In many places the rabbis emphasize the importance of tithes. It is through the merit of tithes that Israelites obtain their desires from God. Through tithing, the Israelites escape the twelve month punishment of the wicked after death. The severity of encroaching on tithe regulation is so severe that anyone who eats fruit of which the tithe for the poor has not been appropriated is deserving of death (Pesiḳ. xi. 99a, b).[53] Finally, the non-payment of tithes brings natural disasters (Midr. Teh. to Ps. Xviii).[54]

3.7 Summary of Findings

The discussion on the codified tithe has shown that the OT has nothing against the principle of tithing. In fact tithing is seen as an obligation which any devout Jew must fulfil although it has no place in the covenant law between God and the sons of Jacob on Sinai. Before the law of tithing came, the sanctuary had been constructed and the Levites have taken their place as the officials of the house of Yahweh. But with the non-allocation of inheritable land to the tribe of Levi, the tithe became the main source of the sustenance of the Levites. The tithe was also helpful so that the widows and poor of the land would have a sure means of survival. It may not be necessary to ask what could have led to poverty in a land supposedly flowing with milk and honey. Poverty was a reality in the life of this folk and means must be put in place to alleviate the effect.

It is often a neglected fact that in the discourse of tithe in the OT, nowhere was the issue of money either stated or implied except when the tithe is to be exchanged to enable the tithe bringer carry the proceeds to the place of worship. Every reference to the payment of tithe both in the OT and rabbinic sources was from the agricultural produce of the

---

[53] Quoted in J. Jacobs/M. Seligsohn/W. Bacher, Jewish Encyclopedia, s.v. "Tithe."
[54] Quoted in J. Jacobs/M. Seligsohn/W. Bacher, Jewish Encyclopedia, s.v. "Tithe." The details have been analyzed by H. Lansdell, Sacred Tenth, 1:120-28.

land or herds. This is understandable since the earth is the Lord's and its fullness. Therefore, any payment of tithe is regarded as nothing but a little return to God the owner of the land. However, this last point has been glossed over by those who argue that the laws of tithe were given during an agrarian period. The argument is that if Moses lived in a more commercialized milieu he would have requested that the tithes be paid with cars, TV sets, etc. In the same vein, a more money-intensive environment could have requested Euros, Dollars or Naira.

But it is our ardent view that the OT content of the tithe should be taken more seriously than is presently the case. This is because the payment of tithe based exclusively on agricultural produce is despite the fact that monetary transaction was already current in the Torah. Long before the issue of tithing became a factor, money was used to buy slaves (Gen 17:12), land (Gen 23:9), to pay for sanctuary dues (Ex 30:13), etc. If God wanted tithes to be paid in money, he would have made it explicit even in the Mosaic era. The paying of tithe from the produce of the land arose because the ancients believed that the gods deserve some form of recompense for the things taken from the earth which rightly belongs to them. In the case of Israel, it became a means of taking care of the workers in God's house.

We have elsewhere[55] argued that many green-horn Christians have abandoned many rites and rituals of the OT but keep clinging to the issue of tithing. The questions we asked in our previous study included the following: How did the Christians manage to convince themselves that the Sabbath should be changed to a Sunday? Is it not mainly because Jesus resurrected on the first day of the week? What about the sacrifices of the Temple? Would any Christian still subscribe to the killing of bulls and rams and smearing of their blood on the altars for the expiation of the peoples' sins? Jesus has made enough sacrifices for us, they argue. Contemporary Christians encourage exogamy while the

---

[55] R. Onyenali, Hebrew Women, 49.

practice of marrying from one's relatives was a common practice in the OT (cf. Gen 20:12; 24:4). Abraham had a child with one of his slave girls when it seemed that Sarah would remain barren (cf. Gen 16:1-4). A Bible-carrying Christian would surely frown at this in this era. Even the all-important circumcision that served as a prerequisite for entrance into the chosen community (cf. Gen 17; Ex 12:48f) was already disempowered during the time of the disciples (cf. Acts 15:1-20). With this massive dropping of some OT rites and ways of life there must be something that makes tithing still attractive to modern day Christians. Perhaps the prophecy of Malachi has much to do with this attraction.

CHAPTER FOUR
THE ALMIGHTY MALACHIAN TITHE (Mal 3:6-12)

In the preceding chapter we have seen that the issue of tithing in Judaism was a divine command arising due to the lack of possession on the part of the Levites. Thus, the tithes paid by the Jewish people served as means of sustenance for the *landless* servants of the sanctuary of Yahweh. The tithes also served as source of aid for the poor, the widows and orphans. If this was the recommendation during the time of Moses, the prophet Malachi took it to an all-time high in his indictment of his people who steal from God by not paying their tithes. This text has been serially misread, misunderstood and mispreached through several centuries by the very people that should be the recipients of the message. The only way to understand the message of Malachi is to understand its context.

4.1 The Remote Context of Malachi 3:6-12

One of the major problems involved in the study of the book of the prophet Malachi is the problem of the historical context. Apart from a few oblique references to his person, he never linked his work to any historical situation. Perhaps, the mention of the overthrow of Edom (1:2-5) is a reference to the reprisal attack of Babylon against those who murdered Gedaliah, the Jewish governor appointed by Nebuchadnezzar the king of Babylon.[1] But the text of Malachi 1:2-5 shows that this context is still a future event and may not be decisive in dating the prophecy of Malachi. Historically, the Nabateans expelled the Edomites in 312 BC which resulted in a racial mixture that gave rise to the Idumeans.[2] It is then possible that what Malachi was referring to would

---

[1] Cf. B. Dahlberg, "Studies in the Book of Malachi," 202.
[2] P. C. Hammond, The Nabataeans, 13.

be in the years before 312 BC. Whether Malachi was making a prediction for the future or a prophecy after the event cannot be ascertained. We know, however, that Malachi was attested as early as the early part of the second century BC.[3] It must have been written some years before that time to accord it any canonical status. Beyond this, nothing could be said with historical certainty. What can be said with certainty is that by the time Malachi was prophesying, the exile was over, the second Temple had been rebuilt and the offerings in the Temple had resumed. This favours a time during the Persian period[4] after the rebuilding of the Temple in 515 BC.[5]

Most of the issues addressed by Malachi centred on various forms of religious irregularities and divorce. These place Malachi in a position in which the second Temple was already rebuilt and flourishing (1:6-11; 2:1-3; 3:1.10). But as Taylor proposes "the excitement and enthusiasm for which the prophets Haggai and Zachariah were the catalysts had waned."[6] Instead of enthusiasm, the era of Malachi was characterized by despair and doubt due to the apparent failure of the prophetic visions of Haggai and Zachariah.[7] This implies that Malachi should be later than the prophets whose special interest was the rebuilding of the Jerusalem Temple. This adequately reinforces the fact that Malachi is the bridge between the OT prophets and the prophets of the NT. If Nehemiah predates Malachi, then we reckon Nehemiah as another literary context for the prophecy of Malachi.[8]

---

[3] Cf. Ben Sirach 48:10, which quotes Malachi 3:23-24. For the dating of Ben Sirach around 180 BC see P. W. Skehan, The Wisdom of Ben Sira, 10, 534.

[4] For analysis of the various contours of Yahwism during the Persian period see D. L. Petersen, Zechariah 9-14 and Malachi: A Commentary, 6-9.

[5] R. A. Taylor, Haggai, Malachi, 205.

[6] R. A. Taylor, Haggai, Malachi, 207.

[7] Cf. A. E. Hill, Dating the Book of Malachi, 83.

[8] There are several parallels in the oracles of Nehemiah and Malachi. In his Zachariah 9-14 and Malachi: A Commentary, 5. D. L. Petersen includes concern for proper ritual behavior (Neh 8:13-18; 13:15-18), the need for both a purified priesthood and a recognized place for the Levites (Neh 13:28-30) and the practice of tithing (Neh 13:10-

The following information from Nehemiah could be of great importance to the understanding of Malachi's tithe pronouncement: "And before this, Eliashib the [high] priest, having the oversight of the chamber of the house of our God, was allied unto Tobiah: And he had prepared for him a great chamber, where previously they laid the grain offerings, the frankincense, and the vessels, and the tithes of the grain, the new wine, and the oil, which was commanded to be given to the Levites, and the singers, and the temple guards; and the offerings of the priests" (Neh 13:4-5). Because Nehemiah wrote after the exile, it is to be accepted that many cultic activities have been stopped within the seventy years of exile when Nehemiah himself was not in Jerusalem (Neh 13:6). It could be the intention of Nehemiah to renew these activities. First, there is mention of a storehouse designated to hold the offerings, the first fruits, and the daily rations of the tithes for the Levites and offerings for the priests who were doing their turns in the Temple. Second, Eliashib, the high priest, had emptied this storehouse and allowed Tobiah, Nehemiah's enemy, to occupy it. Third, the responsibility for this sin fell on the priests, under the leadership of the high priest. This text has all of the components of being the context of Malachi 3:6-12.[9] Appreciating the historical gap between the biblical narratives and the events they describe helps to accept the veracity of the above thesis even though the prophecy of Malachi was penned down shortly before Nehemiah assumed office as governor of Jerusalem.

4.2 The Immediate Context of Malachi 3:6-12

With regard to the immediate context of our chosen text, the following can be said. If we divide the book of Malachi into a series of six sections comprising of interrogations and responses (1:2-5; 1:6-2:9; 2:10-16;

---

14) as the oracles common in both prophets.

[9] For review of scholarly opinion on the dating of Malachi see R. A. Taylor, Haggai, Malachi, 206

2:17-3:5; 3:6-12; 3:13--4:3),[10] we see that the teaching on tithe is located in the fifth section of the prophecy. This particular disputation comes after the announcement of the coming of the Messiah who would prepare the way for the Lord. The purification of the sons of Levi, which the Messiah would effect, has the aim of making the offerings of the priests accepted. This is in line with the accusations of religious corruption levelled against the priestly class, hence the need for their purification. This accusation is already the theme of the prophetic outburst already from 1:6. It seems to be the accusation of the priests that continued till our chosen pericope except with some intermittent accusations of the whole of Judah. But ultimately, the addressees of the whole of the prophetic oracles of Malachi are the sons of Levi. We shall see this more clearly as we analyze the text of Malachi 3:6-12. This explains why the words pronounced by the prophet as the words of Yahweh are in the form of indictment and rebuke against the priestly class. Among other themes, we see the sacrilege of the priestly service (1:6-14),[11] and the sacrilege of the priestly message (2:1-9).[12] However, the last parts of the prophecy present a vision of hope (4:2-6).

---

[10] This division has been made by Wendland, "Linear and Concentric Patterns in Malachi," 113. C. Von Orelli, who used three chapters to divide Malachi came up with the following divisions: 1:1-14 as the complaint of neglect, 2:1-16 as the treachery of the priests and people and 2:17-3:24 as the day of the Lord. See his The Twelve Minor Prophets, 390-404.

[11] Malachi's stress on the importance of sacrifice has led some scholars to regard him less a prophet. Perhaps the most damning comment in this regard comes from B. Duhm. For him, the teaching of Malachi shows that true religion consisted of the sacrificial system. Therefore, if Amos, Isaiah, Micah, Jeremiah, etc. were prophets, Malachi could hardly be considered as one. See his Die Theologie der Propheten, 320. For criticism against this view see P. A. Verhoef, The Books of Haggai and Malachi, 255f.

[12] For in-depth study of the implications of these accusations see L-S Tiemeyer, Priestly Rites and Prophetic Rage, 211-17.

4.3 Text and Analysis of Malachi 3:6-12

As already said above, the text of Malachi 3:6-12 falls within the fifth disputation of the prophetic utterances of Malachi. In the very words of the prophet:

> "For I the Lord do not change; therefore you, O sons of Jacob, are not consumed. From the days of your fathers you have turned aside from my statutes and have not kept them. Return to me, and I will return to you, says the Lord of hosts. But you say, 'How shall we return?' Will man rob God? Yet you are robbing me. But you say, 'How are we robbing thee?' In your tithes and offerings. You are cursed with a curse, for you are robbing me; the whole nation of you. Bring the full tithes into the storehouse, that there may be food in my house; and thereby put me to the test, says the Lord of hosts, if I will not open the windows of heaven for you and pour down for you an overflowing blessing. I will rebuke the devourer for you, so that it will not destroy the fruits of your soil; and your vine in the field shall not fail to bear, says the Lord of hosts. Then all nations will call you blessed, for you will be a land of delight, says the Lord of hosts."

This passage presents one of the many ways through which the addressees have deviated from following divine dictates. It is easy to see how 1:6-2:9 and 3:6-12, in a sense function as companion pieces in that they focus on the neglect of the cult.[13] Both oracles begin with a double-assertion-questioning pattern, followed by a denunciation of unacceptable offerings, the assurance of the turnaround of fortune, and an exaltation of the name Yahweh in all the nations.[14] In this present situation, it seems to be a matter of flagrant self-centredness and

---

[13] L-S Tiemeyer, Priestly Rites and Prophetic Rage, 27.

[14] B. O.Bọlọjẹ/A. Groenewald, Hypocrisy in stewardship. Available at http://www.hts.org.za/index.php/HTS/article/view/2086/4649. Accessed 16.08.2016.

deception from the part of the audience. The introductory verse hints at the inalterable nature of God (v.6). It might be that his forbearance and faithfulness to his covenantal promises[15] have ensured the survival of the listeners to this passage despite all the sins enumerated against them since the beginning of the prophetic book.[16] Hence, the faithfulness of Yahweh and the faithlessness of his people are the two poles of the present discourse. In v.7a there is accusation against the people for their lack of fidelity to the covenant principles. This means that apostasy is the main problem.[17] In a suzerainty treaty, the keeping of the covenant is evidently the function of a vassal.[18] We also see the peoples' query as to why they should return (v.7b). The object of the problem is specified (v.8). This specification complicates the case by bringing out another accusation of robbery (v.8)[19] to that of turning away from the Lord (v.7). Eventually, the double accusation of turning away from Yahweh and robbing him is specified only in the lack of payment of the tithes and the offerings. As already seen, the codified tithe was for the need of the Levites (Num. 18:21.26) and others in need (Deut. 14:26-27; 26:12).[20] But if read in the context of Nehemiah 13, the tithe of the Levites should

---

[15] Cf. N. M. Waldman, "Some Notes on Malachi 3:6; 3:13; and Psalm 42:11," JBL 93 (1974):544.

[16] So also J-A I. van der Merwe, An Exegetical and Theological Study of Malachi 3:8-12, 42.

[17] Also R. E. Clendenen, Malachi, 429.

[18] Cf. Deut. 11:32; 26:17; Ex 19:3-8, etc. The relationship between the Ancient Near Eastern treaties and the Old Testament has been adequately studied by J. A. Thompson, The Ancient Near Eastern Treaties and the Old Testament. London, 1964.

[19] For the different translations of the verb used in this verse to mean cheat or to plunder, see Jo-Anne Iris van der Merwe, An Exegetical and Theological Study of Malachi 3:8-12, 45.

[20] This view is supported by D. O., Wretlind, Shekels, Dollars & Sense, 22. On the other hand, M. A. Sweeney, The Twelve Prophets, 743, considers that this tithe is a reference to the tithe meant for the support of the Levites as listed in Leviticus 27:30-33, Numbers 18:21-32 and Deuteronomy 14:22-29. For D. L. Petersen, Zechariah 9-14 & Malachi, 215 this is the "general tithe." He also holds that this was the tithe collected in local storehouses and designated for the Levites.

be in view here.[21] Withholding the offering of these gifts is tantamount to robbing God (8).[22] The effect of this robbery is that they people are already cursed (v.9a). The nature of the curse is, however, not specified. The depth of the injury is shown in the repetition of the accusation of robbery (v.9b). Despite the depth of this injury and the curse that follows from it, there would be blessing on those who pay their tithe and bring their offerings (vv.10-11). The whole tithe could be a reference to our three kinds of tithes or only to the first tithe meant for the Levites. The tithe is to be brought into the storehouse of Yahweh from where it would be distributed to the needy. The offerings could be a reference to the ritual offerings which the Jews were supposed to offer at the required times. Therefore, the blessings of Yahweh will be for those who pay their tithes and bring other forms of religious offerings. God's blessing will involve rebuking the devourer to the effect that the harvest will surpass the expectation of the people. When this is achieved, other nations will call Judah blessed (v.12).

The pericope can be given a fitting structural pattern.[23]

A[1] Introduction: a divine premise (v.6)

   B[1] Appeal—repent (v.7)

      C[1] Indictment: "you have robbed me" (v.8)

         D Verdict: curse (v.9a)

      C[2] Indictment: "you are robbing me" (v.9b)

   B[2] Promise—blessings on those who repent (v.10-11)

A[2] Conclusion: a messianic vision (v.12)

---

[21] So also J.-A. I. van der Merwe, An Exegetical and Theological Study of Malachi 3:8-12, 45.

[22] E. R. Clendenen, E.R., 2004, 'Malachi', in E.R. Clendenen & R.A. Taylor (eds.), *Haggai, Malachi*, pp. 203–464, Broadman and Holman Publishers, Nashville. (New American Commentary, 21A), 415.

[23] This pattern has been identified by E. Wendland, Linear and Concentric Patterns in Malachi, 118.

With this division, we have a chiastic pattern where the divine premise of v.6 corresponds to the messianic vision of v.12; the appeal to repentance in v.7 and the promise of blessing on those who repent of vv.10-11 form a pair; there is a double indictment of robbery in v.8 and in v.9b. The implication then is that the pronouncement of the curse in v.9a forms the centre-piece of the statement. If our analysis is correct, the oracle of Malachi appears more frightening than previously assumed. The implications must be taken more seriously.

4.4 Implications of Malachi 3:6-12

We have analyzed the context of Malachi as evidence of religious decay and the need to escape divine retribution that accrues from not keeping the injunctions of Yahweh. We have also seen that from 1:6, the addressees of the prophetic oracle were the priests who were supposed to be the custodians of the cult. The invectives used against them indicate that they have failed in their responsibility to God and to the people. It is then logical to infer that the priests were principally the ones cursed for not paying their tithes.[24] Their inability to carry out this obligation affected the whole nation in failing also to pay theirs.[25] This is a conclusion that flows from the logic of the text.

---

[24] For R. Kelly, Should the church teach tithing, especially in chapter 13, the whole of the prophetic oracle was addressed to the priests and not the people in general. His conclusion is derived from many arguments. First, he thinks that in no other place are the whole people told to bring in the whole tithe to the central storehouse. This seems to be the function of the priest in charge of the provisions in the storehouse. Second, it seems that there is no change of addressees identified in the second chapter as the priests. He therefore considers chapter three to be a continuation of the indictment started in chapter two.

[25] Those who conclude that the whole nation is involved in the indictment include R. E. Clendenen, Haggai Malachi. The new American commentary: An exegetical and theological exposition of holy scripture (vol. 21A). Nashville, 2004; D. Stuart, The Minor Prophets: An Exegetical and Expository Commentary (vol. 13). Grand Rapids, (1998); P. C. Craigie, Twelve Prophets: Micah, Nahum, Habbakuk, Zephaniah, Zechariah and Malachi. Louisville, 1985.

However, this conclusion is fraught with some difficulties which might be hard to clarify. First and foremost, our study of the tithe legislation in the OT never showed any requirement from the priests to pay tithes. The much we get to the demand of tithe from cultic officials in the Torah is the injunction that the Levites are to pay a tithe of the tithe they received to the priests (cf. Num 18:26). This means that the priests of the first Temple era received tithes by proxy but never paid any. Even as the second Temple began to flourish, Nehemiah reminds the people of their cultic obligations. They are to bring the prescribed offerings to the priests and the tithes to the Levites (Neh 10:35-39). Again, there is no mention of the priests offering tithes. If the whole nation has reneged on the payment of tithes, it is to be concluded that the Levites are part of those who failed to adhere to this divine mandate.

But how does one justify the argument that the accusation of robbing God affects the priests directly? We refer back to Nehemiah as the literary context for Malachi. At the time of Nehemiah, the house of God was forsaken and the tithes stolen from the chambers. Nehemiah informs us that the High priest Eliashib was in charge of this storehouse (Neh 13:4). This storehouse contained the grain offerings, the frankincense, and the vessels, and the tithes of the grain, the new wine, and the oil, which was commanded to be given to the Levites, and the singers, and the temple guards; and the offerings of the priests. Under the watch of Eliashib, the storehouse was emptied of the offerings for the priests and the tithes that belonged to the Levites. The situation grieved Nehemiah who cleansed the chamber and ordered that the vessels of the house of God, with the grain offering and the frankincense be brought back (Neh 13:8-9). Here, no mention is made of returning the tithes meant for the Levites. It seems that the Levites have been robbed of their tithe. If the High priest was responsible for this robbery as the one in charge of the storehouse, the rhetorical question of Malachi 3:8 receives a new light. Can a man rob God? Therefore, the addressees of Malachi 3:10 would be the priests (or High Priest) who refused to give the Levites their portion of the gifts that were in the storehouse of God.[26] This made the Levites to abandon their responsibilities as stated by Nehemiah: "And I realized that the portions of the Levites had not been given them: for the Levites and the singers, that did the work, were fled everyone to his field" (Neh 13:10). It was Nehemiah who restored the priests and Levites (Neh 13:11-13). With their restoration, the storehouse had to be filled. This seems to be the heart of the Malachian text. This is the way some scholars have interpreted Malachi 3:10.[27] If this is the case, that is, if Nehemiah 13 is the context of Malachi 3:8-10, then it makes flawless logic. The priests, who had already been cursed by God three times in Malachi are the ones receiving another curse here. They had taken care of their own needs while neglecting the Levites. God is thus telling the priests in Malachi 3:10 to bring "all the tithe" that belongs to the empty storeroom back to that storeroom, especially the portion they had stolen from the Levites. If our analysis is correct, we have an ironic situation in which the modern day priests, who should stand in the place of the cursed Eliashib for misappropriation of the Levitical tithes, use the same portion of Scripture to commit further arts of robbery. This is nothing but double divine robbery. It is an aspect of the theology of tithe that should be vigorously investigated.

It is only when one concludes that the nation is cursed for not paying tithes correctly in Malachi 3:9 that tithing becomes a sort of *do ut des*; I give so as to receive. That means if you want to receive from God you first give. This is the main theology of the tithing preached in many Christian gatherings. In this type of preaching, tithe is the instrument to attract God's favours. Absence of the tithe means absence of divine

---

[26] This is also the way J. Williams saw it in his Pimps in the Pulpit, 23. Other scholars who see the divine robbery as the work of Eliashib, the High Priest include the following: J. Suton, Another More Excellent Way, 55f; R. E. Kelly, Should the Church Teach Tithing?, 86.

[27] See also J. Suton, Another More Excellent Way, 55f;

blessings. This is a classical way of creating God in the image and likeness of mere mortals. Anyone who grew up in an environment where material gift is the main instrument to attract favours from the sovereign understands exactly how this functions. The vassal gives gifts in order to be looked with the eyes of favour. In the minds of many, as it is on earth, so it is also in heaven.

But even if one is to accept that the people (laity) were the ones indicted in the oracle of Malachi, the narrative indicates that the accusation is based on neglecting the payment of tithes and the bringing of other offerings. A clearer understanding of the double accusation would require some enquiry into the Jewish sacrificial system.

4.5 Other Forms of Jewish Offering

As seen above, the prophecy of Malachi combines the paying of tithe with the bringing of other forms of offerings. This implies that the paying of the tithe does not exhaust the whole cultic demand of a devout Jew and does not answer to the double indictment of Malachi. The OT presents a complex system of offerings or sacrifices which do not replace the tithes. It could even be argued that these sacrifices have more importance than the tithes.[28] Evidently, "Sacrifice is at the heart of all true worship. It serves as the consecrating ritual for participation in the holy rites, it forms the appropriate tribute due to the LORD, and it represents the proper spiritual attitude of the worshiper."[29] It becomes even more significant when the sacrifice involves blood. This is because in the Jewish religion "blood is a ritual detergent when used by the priests in the Temple in order to purify the sancta after they have been contaminated."[30] The whole system can be simplified in the following

---

[28] A reference to Leviticus 17:11 shows how important blood sacrifice is to the entire Jewish cult. Here the identification of blood with life shows its immense function in the sacrificial system. Cf. W. K. Gilders, Blood Ritual in the Hebrew Bible: Meaning and Power. London, 2004.

[29] Allan P. Ross, Holiness to the LORD, 73.

forms of sacrifices: (1) Holocaust or burnt offering (olah), (2) Common or peace offering (selamin) and (3) Expiatory offering (hatta't and asam).

4.5.1 Holocaust or Burnt Offering (olah)

The Holocaust or Burnt Offering (olah) is derived from the Hebrew alah which literally means an offering of ascent or a sacrifice that is taken up to God. it was the commonest of all the OT sacrifices.[31] It can also be seen as the sacrifice which goes up to God. Since the sacrifice is entirely consumed by the fire of the altar (apart from the skin of the victim), it is called olah. In some places, the kalil or total sacrifice serves as alternative term for the olah (cf. 1 Sam 7:9; Deut 33:10; cf. Ps 51:21).[32] It is the LXX that gave it the translation of o`loka,rpwsij, that is, "holocaust". It is called holocaust (wholly burnt) in Greek because the whole victim is burnt except the skin. Since the sacrifice is entirely burnt on the altar, the smoke was directed towards the abode of God. The inhaling of the scent by God was the object of this sacrifice. This was seen as the highest of the offerings that could be presented to God. It was an offering of the entire person of the offerer to God (Ps. 40:8f; Heb. 10:5f). We find instances of this form of sacrifice in Deut 33:10; I Sam 7:9.

Unlike the tithe which functions as thanksgiving to God for the gift of the land, this form of offering is for the forgiveness of sins. The sins expiated by the olah are not specified in the Hebrew Scriptures. But it seems that the Holocaust is all-embracing as it answers to every kind of offence that is not covered by the other forms of sacrifice like hatta't and the asam which expiate the limited sins of the pollution and

---

[30] D. Biale, Blood and Belief: The Circulation of a Symbol Between Jews and Christians, 10. Another reference to an indepth study of blood sacrifice in the OT is the work of J. Milgrom in Leviticus 17-22 (AncB). New York, 2000.

[31] Cf. G. J., Wenham, The Book of Leviticus (NICOT), 63.

[32] R. De Vaux, Ancient Israel,.415

desecration of sacred things.[33] Although the Law prescribes that the victim of the burnt offering must be a male animal without any blemish (cf. the Law of Holiness, Lev 22:17-25) or a bird (though only a turtle-dove or a pigeon), the Holocaust victim was often accompanied with cereal and drink offerings (Num 15: 1-10).

The importance of ritual purity in Judaism is also shown in the Law related to this offering since the man making the offering must be in a state of ritual purity. By presenting the victim and laying his hands on the head of the victim, he implies that the victim is a substitute for him. By this symbolic action, his sins are transferred to the victim. Therefore, the merits of the sacrifice accrue to him.[34] It is the death of the sacrificial victim that renders the rite effective, and the manipulation of the blood highlights the death that stands in the place of the sinner who offers it.[35] There is no way such ritual of immense value can be overlooked in the Jewish religion.

4.5.2 The Peace Offering (*selamin*).

This sacrifice is best introduced with these important remarks from G. Bush:

> "The word peace has a different shade of meaning in the Hebrew from what it has in our language. With us it suggests most naturally and legitimately the idea of reconciliation, the bringing into concord contending parties,—an idea which is more properly to be associated with the effects of the stated burnt-offering, or the occasional sin and trespass-offering. In the Hebrew the

---

[33] J. Milgrom, Sacrifices and offerings,769; M. F. Rooker, Leviticus, 85..

[34] R. De Vaux, *An Ancient Israel*, Its Life and Institutions, London: Redwood Books, 1961, 416

[35] Longman and Dillard, *An Introduction to the Old Testament*. 2nd ed. Grand Rapids: Zondervan, 2006.
86.

import of prosperity, of welfare, is prominant [sic] to the enjoyment of the petition of which this offering was especially appointed. The idea of grateful acknowledgment therefore is the leading idea which it is calculated to suggest."[36]

The whole essence of the above citation is that the idea of gratitude for favours received is at the back of this offering. Its main focus is not the reconciliation of contending parties but the offering of gratitude to God. Generally, the selamin is the basic form of sacrifice presented on feast days (1 Sam 1:3-4; Deut 12:11-12). It is a sacrifice of thanksgiving to God for being saved from death and being granted a new life. Very similar to the *selamin* are the *pesah* "Passover," and "ordination" sacrifices.

The *selamin* is divided into three sub-types in the P source (e.g. Lev 7:11-18). We have the following sub-types: (1) The *toda* or "thanksgiving" sacrifice; (2) the *neder "vowed* sacrifice," and (3) the *nedaba* "freewill offering." For the accomplishment of the *selamin,* various victims are presented for various sacrifices. From the herd a male or female without blemish is chosen (Lev 3:1-5); from the flock, a male or female without blemish (Lev 3:6-11). The victim could also be a goat (Lev 3:12-17). Sometimes, grain made into a cake with oil and a wine libation accompanied the sacrifice (Num 15:7-12) of every bull, lamb, or kid.

The victim is shared between God and the people. This is the only sacrifice in which the offerer shares in eating the victim. However, the choicest parts of the victim are given to the priest (Lev 7:30-34). As a thanksgiving sacrifice, it can be related to the Eucharist of the Catholic Church (cf. 1Cor 5:7-8; 10:16-18; 11:23-26; Col 1:20). According to Exod 12: 9, it is a sacrifice that all Israel must consume. Unlike the other selamin offerings, the *pesah,* and *toda* sacrifices were all to be eaten on the very day they were offered. The fact that the flesh of the victim must

---

[36] G. Bush, Notes, 33.

be consumed within one day points to a higher level of sanctity.[37] The meal is to cement the relationship between God and the participants.[38] Since the people are to share in this sacrifice they are supposed to observe prescribed rituals of purity.

4.5.3 The Expiatory Sacrifices (hatta't and asam)

The Expiatory sacrifices are divided into two: (1) the hatta't and (2) the *asam.* The hatta't is the purification offering while the asam is the reparation offering.

a. **Purification Offering** (hatta't). The aim of the hatta't is to atone for sins committed un-knowingly, especially where no restitution was possible (Lev 4: 1-5:13, Num 1 5:22-31). The act of sacrifice serves to purge or purify something rather than to remove sin. It does not only purify the offerer but also the sanctuary.[39] It also purifies the High priest (Lev 4:3-12), the congregation (Lev 4:13-21), the ruler, (Lev 4:22-26), a commoner, (Lev 4:27-35). In cases of poverty, two turtledoves or two young pigeons (one for a sin offering, the other for a burnt offering) could be substituted (Lev 5:7-9). In cases of extreme poverty, fine flour could be substituted (Lev 6:11-13). The sacrifice is performed in rituals that have an atoning function. The blood is understood as a purifying agent. The purification rite is performed so that the sinner may be forgiven (Lev 4: 20, 26, 31).

(b). **Reparation Offering** (asam). This offering is often translated as "guilt offering." The main reference to the asam is Lev 5:14ff. The procedure of the sacrifice is given in Lev 7:1-7. The meaning "reparation offering" can be adduced from the unique accompanying verbs, "restore" (Num 5:-7-8; 18:9; 1 Sam 6:3-4, 17) and "repay" (Lev

---

[37] J. Finegan, Light from the Ancient Past, 51.

[38] The slain-offering [peace offering], which culminated in the sacrificial meal, served as a seal of the covenant fellowship, and represented the living fellowship of man with God. See C. F., Keil/F. Delitzsch. The Pentateuch (vols.2), 268.

[39] J. Milgrom, Sacrifices and offerings, 766.

6:5).[40] Unlike other sacrifices which one offers, the asam can be converted into a monetary equivalent and simply be paid (Lev 5:15, 18; 6:6).

Apart from these classical Jewish offerings, there are also the daily sacrifices, the remembrance sacrifices, the sacrifices on the new moon, etc. Although the text of Malachi 3:6-12 did not specify on these sacrifices, the indictment on the priests and the people about robbing God in their tithes and offerings (Mal 3:8) could be a reference to all these forms of sacrifices. Any intention to respond accurately to the Malachian mandate should be a response and a return to these ancient sacrifices. This is a return that should be considered by every ardent follower of the Jewish scriptures. Otherwise the focus on tithe alone as the correct approach to Malachi 3:6-12 is a misplacement of emphasis.

4.6 Tithing in Modern Judaism

Most of the arguments in the previous parts of this book have been geared towards the desire of Christians to appropriate the dictates of the OT. This is understandable since the Christians possess the double heritage of the two testaments.[41] We have already seen the meaning and the why of the command to pay a tenth of the proceeds of the land which belongs to God. The main reason behind this command was to cater for the needs of those who ministered in the house of God, especially, the Levites and also to take care of the needy. A further need was to take care of communal celebrations of the cult.

However, with the destruction of the first temple in 587 BC by the army of Nebuchadnezzar II after the Siege of Jerusalem, every form of

---

[40] J. Milgrom, Sacrifices and offerings, 768.

[41] But as C. U. Manus argues, there is a great span of 4000 years between the modern day pastors and the OT biblical texts they preach from. There is also massive temporal gap between the writing of the biblical texts and the events they narrate. Failure to acknowledge this leads to failure to appreciate the importance of contextual interpretation of the bible. See his Tithing, 147f.

sacrifice or offering in the Temple and to the Temple officials ceased. With the rebuilding of the Temple in 516 BC and its dedication the following year, normal Temple activities resumed. This second Temple was in existence during the time Jesus walked the streets of Palestine. It was in this Temple that he was presented (Lk 2:22), and was found teaching the teachers of the Law (2:41-48). It was also this Temple that he cleansed and prophesied its destruction (Mt 24:2). Although he paid the half shekel (Mt 17:27),[42] we were not told that he or any of his disciples paid any form of tithe. It is possible that during this time, the payment of tithe was voluntary and practiced only by the Pharisees (Lk 18:12). In fact, in the year 70 AD, this Temple was destroyed and has not been rebuilt again. Although some Jews tried to renew some sort of the Jewish offerings during the revolt of Bar Koch bar, the crushing of this revolt by the Romans ensured the end of Jewish sacrifice. Nonetheless, pious Jews still await the coming of the Messiah who would rebuild the Temple and ensure the continuity of the offerings or the Korbanot as they are classically called. Already, priests are being prepared for the administration of the third Temple when it is rebuilt.

Meanwhile, the practice of tithing has gone into oblivion in the Jewish religion. Those to whom the command to tithe was given and who still realize the meaning of the tithe understand that without the presence of those legally ordained as priests and Levites in Judaism, it is illegal to pay or receive tithes from anyone. Surely, there are still rabbis in every community where the Jewish religion has scattered since the destruction of the second Temple. They perform the functions of instructing the people in the ways of Yahweh. Yet the refrain from collecting tithes since they understand that doing so will be stealing from Yahweh, the owner of the tithes. Instead of depending on tithe for

---

[42] A half shekel was levied by Moses on the people for furnishing the Tabernacle. On the return from captivity, the people charged themselves with contributing the third part of a shekel for servicing the house of God (cf. Neh 10:32).

their sustenance, they engage in normal lifestyle like every other pious Jew.

4.7 Summary of Findings

We have gone through the historical context and the theology of Malachi 3:6-12. We have seen the reason behind Malachi's prophetic outburst as not limited to the issue of tithe but also related to the overall deviation from the law of Yahweh by the whole nation. Yet, the people at the centre of Malachi's attrition were the priests who were involved in various forms of religious irregularities. He attacks them personally. It seems that the sin of the people is that they have followed the priests in falling away from the covenantal commitments. We have also seen how the payment of tithes and other offerings could be at the heart of the divine anger. The tithes and other forms of sacrifices or offerings were at the heart of the Jewish religion before the two destructions of the Temple in Jerusalem. With the destruction of the first and second Temples, the practice of ritual sacrifice and the system of tithing seem to have become important for students of Jewish history.

But as has been adequately shown in this chapter, the issue of ritual sacrifice seems to be more at the heart of the Jewish religion than the issue of tithing. This could be seen in the expiatory and purificatory functions of the sacrifices. It is also shown in the fact that for a pious Jews to partake of the sacrificial banquet he or she is supposed to be in a state of ritual purity. This could be called the state of grace in contemporary theology. No other period do the Abrahamic religions require this sort of teaching than now where religious practices have been devoid of any form of morality. Ours is a time when people pay their tithes and forget any form of morality. They seem to argue that they have bought their salvation with their monetary gifts. Little wonder our society is the way it is today.

Question to the reader: Is there any justification for eliminating the other ritual offerings of Jewish religion while retaining the tithe?

CHAPTER FIVE
THE NEW TESTAMENT TITHE

The question posed to the reader towards the end of the fourth chapter could be easily answered in this chapter. This is because various verses of the NT make references to this vestige of the OT cultic demand. Before discussing the particular references to tithe in the NT, it is our wish to make a quick discourse of the general attitude of Jesus towards some of the 613 Laws of Moses. To a large extent, understanding this relationship might help the reader to understand the Christian application of the Laws of Moses to the church.

5.1 The New Testament and the Mosaic Law

It is evident that various kinds of "muddled thinking and unexamined assumptions"[1] abound in the treatment of the subject of the relationship between the OT and the new era. While some of the Laws are accepted as timeless and eternal, some are relegated to the backwater of archaic narrative. For example, the command to love one's neighbour as oneself (Lev 19:18) is regarded as timeless.[2] The next command in the very same verse forbidden the wearing of clothing woven from two different materials is considered irrelevant in modern times. Again, the condemnation of homosexuality in Lev 20:13 continues to function as argument for Christians to challenge the new wave of gay movements,

---

[1] C. E. B. Cranfield, "St Paul and the Law," SJT 17 (1964), 43.

[2] The love of neighbour, together with the love of God is seen as the summary of all the laws by NT authors. See Mt 22:37-40; Mk 12:30-33; Rom 13:9-10; Gal 5:4; Jam 2:8. However, what many scholars normally forget is that the OT idea of neighbour is quite different from the NT application of the same term. While the OT sees one's neighbour as an Israelite or resident alien (cf. Ex 22:20; Deut 10:19), the NT regards the whole of mankind as falling under the spectrum of neighbour because of the universality of Christ's salvific death (cf. Rom 8:32; 2 Cor 5:14-15; 1 Tim 2:4-6; Heb 2:9).

yet the other commands in the same chapter, including the prohibition against the eating of unclean animals (Lev 20:25) and the death sentence on anyone who curses his father or mother (Lev 20:9) are seen as outdated. The inconsistency in Christian exegesis with regard to the acceptance of the injunctions of Deut. 22:5 has been noted by G. D. Fee and D. Stuart.[3] The inconsistency lies in the fact that this same passage stipulates that a woman should not wear man's clothing or a man a woman's. Further, we read that one should not build a parapet around the roof of one's new house (v.8), that one should not plant two kinds of seeds in a vineyard (v.9) and that the wearing of tassels on the four corners of one's cloak is prohibited (v.12). But while arguments still rage in many quarters about the correct feminine clothing, no one seems to bother about the other stipulations in the passage.

The life of Jesus also shows some level of ambivalence with regard to the Mosaic stipulations. With his presentation in the Temple and the presentation of offerings according to the Law of Moses (Lk 2:22-39), his submission to John's baptism so as to fulfil all righteousness (Mt 3:15),[4] his comment that he has come to fulfil the Law (Mt 5:17)[5] and his command to the cured leper to "show yourself to the priest and offer the sacrifices that Moses commanded for your cleansing, as a testimony to them" (Lk 5:14), one gets the impression that Jesus fully applied himself to the observance of the Laws of Moses. It is on this basis that covenant theologians argue that the New Testament is the continuation of the Old and that we do not have two covenants but one covenant. But a certain level of ambivalence appears with regard to his declaring all foods clean (cf. Mk 7:19). However, we shall devote a section to analyzing this passage to see the context of such abolition of the Law he has come to fulfil.

---

[3] G. D. Fee/D. Stuart, How to Read the Bible, 19.

[4] For the whole import of the term "righteousness" in Matthew's gospel see G. Schrenk, "δικαιοσύνη" ThWNT II.200f.

[5] Did Jesus include the food laws of Leviticus chapter 11?

Meanwhile, the NT itself manifests a certain aversion for the Jewish Laws. We read in Acts 15:22-29 that the Council of Jerusalem ruled against the Judaizers who demanded that the gentile converts to Christianity must be circumcised before they could become authentic followers of Jesus. In the case of Paul, we see an unrepentant attack on the Mosaic Law.[6] Although he declared the goodness of the Law in many passages,[7] his main line of argument seems to be a rejection of some of the core principles of the Jewish religious system. Paul argued against the demand on the Christians in Galatia to observe special days and months and seasons and years (Gal 4:10). His submission is that anyone who allowed himself to be circumcised has no part in Christ (Gal 5:2). Writing to the Colossians, he enjoined them not to allow anyone to judge them in what they eat or drink or with regard to a religious festival, a New Moon celebration or the Sabbath (Col 2:16). Although there are varied opinions among Pauline scholars as to the full import of the Pauline arguments against the law, a concrete citation might give insight as to the direction of Paul's argument. Writing to the Galatians he mentions "works of the Law" three times in a verse:

> know that a person is not justified by the works of the law, but by faith in Jesus Christ. So we, too, have put our faith in Christ Jesus that we may be justified by faith in Christ and not by the works of the law, because by the works of the law no one will be justified (Gal 2:16).

---

[6] There is rich literature on the Pauline view of the Jewish Law. Among the important ones, the following readily come to mind: R. K. Rapa, The Meaning of "Works of the Law" in: Galatians and Romans (StudBL 31), New York, 2001; J. K. Hardin, Galatians and the Imperial Cult (WUNT 2. R 237), Tübingen, 2008; M. Hietanen, Paul's Argumentation in Galatians: A Pragma-Dialectical Analysis (Library of New Testament Studies 344, New York, 2007; P. C. Onwuka, The Law, Redemption and Freedom in Christ: An Exegetical-Theological Study of Galatians 3,10-14 and Romans 7,1-6 (TGST 156), Roma, 2007; T. A. Wilson, The Curse of the Law and the Crisis in Galatia: Reassessing the Purpose of Galatians (WUNT 2. R 225), Tübingen, 2007.

[7] See for instance Rom 3:31; 7:12-14; I Cor 9:8-10.

For us to understand the precise meaning of "works of the Law" in this passage we have to refer to the context. This verse is written after some incidents which Paul has referred to in this letter. He has already mentioned the incident in Jerusalem which concerned circumcision (Gal 2:2-4) and the incident with Peter in Antioch which concerned clean and unclean food (Gal 2:11-14). One can then conclude that "Paul uses the expression to refer to the practice of those laws that Peter and other observant Jews consider so important that they force them to separate from the people who accord less importance to these laws, be they Christians of Gentile origin who are not circumcised, or Christians of Jewish origin who have abandoned the dietary laws, as Peter did before changing his opinion."[8]

In the history of the church, the realization, in some quarters of the difficulty involved in applying the teachings of the OT to the life of the Christian led to many forms of heresies. We are allowed here to refer to dispensationalism as one of these heresies. The basic teaching of dispensationalism is captured in the following lines: "only those portions of the bible which are directly addressed to the child of God under grace are to be given a personal or primary application…it does not follow that the Christian is appointed by God to conform to those governing principles which were the will of God for people of other dispensations."[9] One is thus faced with the problem of choosing from the corpus of OT revelation what should be applicable to the Christian. It is to be wondered how one would arrive at an objective choice.

Another heresy that rocked the church in the second century was marcionism. The apparent strict nature of the God of the OT and the apparent liberal nature of the God of the NT led Marcion to reject the entire OT with its laws and teachings. He regarded the God of the OT as

---

[8] P. G. Martinez, The Dead Sea Scrolls, 55-56.
[9] See L. S. Chafer, Major Bible Themes, 97.

being inferior to the God of the NT.[10] Hence the OT laws are not worthy to be obeyed by Christians.[11] Also the many apparent contradictions he found in the OT made him to remove any OT references in the NT from his canon of the NT. Marcion even argued that the NT, especially the gospels, is contaminated as it contains the Jewish adulteration of the true message of Jesus. This contamination made Jesus to appoint Paul to begin afresh the teaching of the true gospel. This means that only the letters of Paul contain the authentic Christian message.[12] From his reading of Galatians 1:12 he concluded that there was only one gospel, that given to Paul. Every other preacher, including those who accompanied the earthly Jesus was preaching a false gospel.

One can only conclude that some of these heresies arose because of one-sided reading of the Scriptures. Let us now examine closely Jesus' relationship with the Jewish Laws. We shall use the text of Mk 7:19 to prove the insight of our investigation.

5.2 Jesus and the Laws of Moses with Focus on Mk 7:19

The level of Jesus' participation in the Judaism of his day has been a source of debate for Christian historians and biblicists for many generations. While many accept that Jesus shared in the apocalyptic or messianic expectations of his time, they draw a line with regard to his relation to the purity laws of Judaism. The majority opinion is that Jesus broke with the purity laws of Judaism in his universal call to salvation. For some, the repudiation of the purity laws of the Torah was at the heart of the Jesus' movement. His aim was to form "a community not based on the ethos and politics of purity, but by the ethos and politics of

---

[10] How Marcion's dualism was received by some church fathers has been discussed by E. C. Blackman, Marcion and his Influence, 66-71.

[11] For a fuller discussion on Marcion see A. von Hanack, Marcion: Das Evangelium vom fremden Gott (2nd ed). Leipzig, 1924; E. C. Blackman, Marcion and his Influence. London, 1948; J. Knox, Marcion and the New Testament. Chicago, 1942.

[12] E. C. Blackman, Marcion and his Influence, 42.

compassion."[13] It is argued that Jesus fought against purity codes and the Temple[14] because they were morally and socially anathema.[15] This seems to be correct according to the gospel narratives. In the writings of the evangelists, Jesus ate with sinners, touched lepers[16] and incorporated the outcasts into his ministry (Mt 9:9). In his company were a handful of women who provided for his needs out of their means (Lk 8:1-3). Finally he challenged the ritual paraphernalia of the Temple (cf. Mk 11:15-17//Mt 21:12-13//Lk 19:45). This is the broad outline of the events that earned him enmity from the Jewish establishment and eventually led him to the cross.

However, a hasty acceptance that Jesus declared all foods clean in Mk 7:19 stems from a neglect of the scenario that led to the assertion. The story began with the Pharisees pointing out to Jesus that some of the disciples were eating with unwashed hands (Mk 7:1-2). This means that the disputation is not about clean and unclean food but about the proper way of eating. What many commentators have failed to point out is that the remark that some of the followers of Jesus were eating with unwashed hands is a clear indication that Jesus and some of the disciples were following the ritual code of hand washing. Mark goes on to narrate how the Pharisees would not eat without washing their hands, the cups, pots, vessels and tables according to the traditions of the elders (vv.3-4). This means that what is at stake is not the Law of Moses but the scribal additions or accretions traditionally referred to as the *Halakhot* or tradition of the elders. Surely, the tradition of the elders is not to be identified with the laws of the OT. This is because the Pharisees have added to the laws given to Moses, laws which other Jewish sects like the Sadducees refused to accept.[17] This explains why Jesus accuses them of

---

[13] M. Borg, Meeting Jesus, 49.
[14] N. T. Wright, The New Testament and the People of God. Minneapolis, 1992
[15] J. D. Crossan, The Historical Jesus, 335.
[16] Cf. Mt 8:2-3; Mk 1:40-42; Lk 5:12-13.
[17] This puts the addition of "and all the Jews" (v.3) into question.

spreading the doctrine of men while neglecting the commandment of God (vv.6-7). Here we see the contrast between God's command and human teaching. These verses introduce Isaiah 29:13.[18] This accusation is expanded in vv.8-13. The distinction that Jesus makes between the command of God and the tradition of the elders makes the disciples to ask for the explanation of the parable (v.17). The response points out that what defiles a person is what comes out from a person and not what goes inside (vv.18-23). It is here that we meet the core of our disputation. Exactly in v.19 it is assumed that Jesus declared all foods clean. The observant reader might wonder how the discourse jumped from a discussion on the washing of hands to a conclusion on the purity of foods. Something is missing somewhere and this is where some English translations of the verse might give some insight to the *original* conclusion of this discussion.

New International Version "For it doesn't go into their heart but into their stomach, and then out of the body." (In saying this, Jesus declared all foods clean.)

English Standard Version "since it enters not his heart but his stomach, and is expelled?" (Thus he declared all foods clean.)

New American Standard Bible "because it does not go into his heart, but into his stomach, and is eliminated?" (Thus He declared all foods clean.)

King James Version "Because it entereth not into his heart, but into the belly, and goeth out into the draught, purging all meats?"

The most obvious fact in these translations is that the clause that Jesus declared all foods clean is retained in brackets. This is evidence that the translators found this verse as secondary addition by NT scribes.[19] This

---

[18] For E. Haenchen, the absence of the contrast between God's command and human teaching in the Hebrew text of Isaiah 29:13 shows that Mk 7:6-7 has made use of the LXX, an indication that the verse cannot be attributed to the historical Jesus. See his Der Weg, 262.

[19] There is a more technical explanation to Mk 7:19b which we prefer to add as a

then explains the omission of the clause by the Kings James version which is one of the oldest English translations of the bible. Again, the Codex Sinaiticus does not contain this particular phrase. Written in the fourth century, the Codex Sinaiticus and the Codex Vaticanus feature as the most reliable of the ancient manuscripts. Therefore, it was from the younger and less reliable manuscripts that many translators of Mark's gospel found the parenthetical remark that Jesus declared all foods clean. Many ancient and modern commentators also agree to this conclusion that Jesus declared all foods clean.[20] R. H. Gundry reached the impossible conclusion that "it is the prerogative of Jesus as God's son to change the Law."[21] With the evidence of Mt 5:17-19, Gundry has set up Jesus against Jesus.

Another argument to explain that this declaration of all foods clean is not a dominical saying is the incident in Antioch between Peter and Paul (Gal 2:11). The argument here was whether Jewish Christians should be allowed to eat non-kosher food. It is to be wondered why none of the parties appealed to the words of Jesus in Mk 7:19 as basis for declaring all foods clean. The only logical conclusion is that "the Marcan passage

---

footnote. It is to be noted that there is a textual variant with regard to the word καθαρίζω katharizo (to make clean). The Textus Receptus which follows the later manuscripts renders the clause καταρίζον πάντα τὰ βρώματα where the verb καταρίζον is parsed as neuter participle. On the other hand, the older manuscripts have καταρίζων πάντα τὰ βρώματα. Here the verb is a masculine participle. It is possible that the scribes who wrote the later manuscripts changed the verb form because they did not understand the subject of the verb. If the toilet ἀθεδρών is the subject of the verb, then the masculine form is correct. From a text critical point of view we naturally accept the verdict of the older manuscripts not just because of their age but because they agree more with the logic of the argument. In this case the translation of Mk 7:18-19 would be: "and he said to them, 'are you so lacking in understanding also? Do you not understand that whatever goes into the man from outside cannot defile him, because it does not go into his heart, but into his stomach, and goes out into the toilet, cleansing all foods?'" This is well reflected in the translation of the King James Version.

[20] See for instance, D. J. Rudolph, "Yeshua and the Dietary Laws," 97-98; J. D. G. Dunn, Jesus, Paul and the Law, 45.

[21] R. H. Gundry, Mark, 356.

declaring all foods clean reflects the controversies over Jewish practice in Mark's post-70 C. E. Gentile community much more clearly than any issues we can plausibly situate in Jesus' own mission to fellow Jews around 30 C. E."[22]

Finally, Matthew's failure to add the declaration of all foods clean in his own account of the same story (cf. Mt 15:17-20), is a supporting argument that the declaration in Mark is a scribal comment. Although many scholars have seen this Matthean omission as a reflection of his high regard for the Jewish Law,[23] it is also possible that his version of the story recounts the original ending of the pericope. In this sense, what Jesus set aside was the scribal outgrowths to the Laws of the Torah and not the Mosaic Law per se.

If we turn to the gospel according to John, we have some latent evidence that Jesus was not an outlaw.[24] He went to Jerusalem for pilgrimages, especially during the festivals. John mentions fives journeys: two during the Passover (2:13; 11:15), one during the sukkot

---

[22] P. Fredriksen, Did Jesus Oppose the Purity Laws? Bible Review XI.3 (1995), 18-25, and 42-47. In many other articles, Fredriksen went on to argue that Paul was more adherent to the Jewish Laws than traditionally accepted. See her "Judaizing the Nations: The Ritual Demands of Paul's gospel." NTS 56, (2010), 232-252; "Why Should a 'Law-Free' Mission mean a 'Law-Free' Apostle?" JBL 134, no.3 (2015), 637-650.

[23] Cf. R. Onyenali, Trilogy of Parables, 233. On Matthew's acceptance of the Jewish laws see M. Goulder, "Matthew's Vision," 27; S. Brown, "The Matthean Community," 218; U. Luz, Studies in Matthew, 13f; G. Barth, "Matthew's Understanding," 71; W. D. Davies/D. C. Allison, Matthew I. 501; J. Overman, Gospel, 88f; D. A. Hagner, Matthew, II.104; M. Konradt, Israel, 380f.

[24] This is despite countless studies that depict John's gospel as anti-Semitic. The use of the word oi[ ]Ioudai?oi which appears some seventy times in the gospel to describe the Jews is seen by many as exemplification of the Johannine case against the Jews. See the studies of R. Bultmann, The Gospel of John, 86; S. Sandmel, Anti-Semitism in the New Testament? 101; M. J. Cook, "The Gospel of John and the Jews," Rev Exp 84 (Spring 1987). However, Cook cautions that we should not make too much out of John's use of the term since the fourth evangelist has merely taken over the term as a "symbol of unbelief or disbelief in the platform John is espousing." The Gospel of John and the Jews, 268.

(7:10), one during the festival of dedication (10:22) and one during an unspecified feast (5:1). It is to be supposed that Jesus kept the purity laws for him to participate in the Jewish festivals. This is because participation in the feasts required ritual purification. One might argue that Jesus could have taken part in the feasts without being in a state of ritual purity. But this would be tantamount to accusing Jesus of hypocrisy since he had taught the need for this inner cleansing before bringing ones offering into the Temple (cf. Mt 5:23-24). Thus we have a little insight to Jesus' idea of the ritual laws of Judaism. If Jesus did not observe ritual purity, his accusation of hypocrisy against the Jewish leaders would be a self-caricature. But if Jesus did not destroy these laws, how does that affect his teaching on tithing?

5.3 Tithing in New Testament Times

The beginning of our discussions in this book points to the need to study the word of God in context. This has been the guiding principle of the entire work. It is a historical fact that during the time of Jesus' earthly life, Judah or the whole of the Jewish nation was under the yoke of Roman rule. Under the Roman regime, the Empire did not mandate the Jews to oblige to all the Jewish tenets since it was not operating a theocracy. It is possible that some of the Jews may have used this opportunity to stop the payment of the required tenth of their possession. This laxity could have affected many other forms of the Jewish rituals. This could explain the various Jewish sects during the Roman period as various levels of continued adherence to the Mosaic Laws.[25] If we

---

[25] Excellent works on the Jewish sects have been done. Those on the Pharisees include: J. Neusner, The Rabbinic Traditions about the Pharisees before 70, 3 vols. (Leiden, 1971); E. Rivkin, "Defining the Pharisees: The Tannaitic Sources," HUCA 40-41 (1969-1971): 205-249; idem, A Hidden Reuolution (Nashville, TN, 1978); idem, "Scribes, Pharisees, Lawyers, Hypocrites: A Study in Synonymity," HUCA 49 (1978): 135-142; M. Simon, Jewish Sects at the Time of Jesus (trans. James H. Farley), Philadelphia, 1967, 27-43; L. Finkelstein, The Pharisees: The Sociological Background of Their Faith, (3rd ed.), Philadelphia, 1962, 1:75-76; E. Schiirer, The History of the

regard the parable of Lk 18:9-14 as depicting a historical event that is normative, then the Pharisees seem to have been ardent in paying the tithes. Many instances in the gospels point to the fact that the Pharisees regarded Jesus as one of their own. Some of them brought Jesus to dine with them (Lk 11:37). It was a group of the Pharisees that came to warn him about the deadly plans of Herod on him (Lk 13:31). The Sadducees also seem to revere him for he went into the house of a chief priest to eat bread on the Sabbath (Lk 14:1). Even the Roman centurion who called on Jesus to heal his servant recognized that Jesus was a Jew who kept the ritual ordinances (cf. Lk 7:6). It is also possible that the parents of Jesus took their third tithe to Jerusalem while doing the annual pilgrimage. In this case, there is no way Jesus would have pretended not to be at home with the tithing principles of Judaism. But the question whether Jesus paid tithes or not is never fully answered in the New Testament writings.

When we turn our attention to the broad outline of Jesus' teaching on giving, it is easy to see how he encouraged generosity in giving (Mt 5:42; Lk 3:11; Lk 6:38; Mt 10:8) and also in performing other religious duty of alms giving (Lk 12:33; Mt 6:23; Mt 25:35). In one instance, Jesus seems to have taught that his followers should give more than the required tithe. He told the rich young man to sell everything he has and give the money to the poor in order to have treasures in heaven (Mt 19:16-21). With regard to the issue of tithing, we find only a single instance of Jesus' mentioning tithe as reported by the evangelists: "Woe to you, scribes and Pharisees, hypocrites! for you tithe mint and dill and cummin, and have neglected the weightier matters of the law, justice and mercy and faith; these you ought to have done, without neglecting the others. You blind guides, straining out a gnat and swallowing a camel"

Jewish People in the Age of Jesus Christ (trans. and ed. G. Vermes/F. Millar/M. Black/M. Goodman (3 vols.), Edinburgh, 1973-1987, 2:381-403; E. P. Sanders, Jewish Law from Jesus to the Mishnah, London, 1990.

(Mt 23:23f//Lk 11:42). What the Pharisees are reported to be tithing in this passage are in keeping with the Mishna.[26] While the Mint and the Dill are sweet-smelling herbs used to season food by the Jews, the Cummin is a herb used also by the Jews in seasoning food and in medicine. Obviously Jesus did not disapprove of these minute pharisaic details of the payment of tithe although there is a hint of caricature of their minuteness in naming these three food seasoners. One could conclude from this text that he approved the payment of tithe. However, he pointed out the presence of other wealthier matters of the Law, like justice, mercy and faith. This means that justice, mercy and faith are more important than tithing.

Surprisingly, Jesus also mentioned only agricultural products among the things that the Jewish leaders pay their tithes on. No mention is made of monetary payment. It is also interesting that those referred to as performing this tithing were the religious leaders of that time and not the masses. If Jesus enjoined his followers to do what the Pharisees teach them (Mt 23:2-3), and not to practice what they do, concluding whether he enjoined his disciples to pay the tithe would be difficult to determine since the Pharisees both taught the principles of tithing, as shown in the Mishna, and also performed them as is evident from the gospels. But the great wealth of the second Temple and of the Sadducees in charge of it could be an indication of a wide source of revenue to the Temple of which the tithe could be part of. This is not explicit. But if Jesus did not come to abolish the Law or the prophets, if Jesus did not give any new laws concerning murder, theft or adultery but deepened them, it is then logical to think that he even commanded a deeper level of giving to God than what the Law of Moses laid down. The words of H. Lansdell are worthy of recalling: "…Neither, again, did the Lord re-enact that His followers should pay a patriarchal tithe, a Levitical tithe, a festival tithe, a poor's tithe, a demai tithe, or any other; but so far was he from

---

[26] Cf. Mishna Masseroth, ch iv, sect. vi.

repealing the law concerning tithes, or lowering God's claims on property, that he set before those who would be his followers a more complete fulfilment of God's law...."[27]

We get confirmation of this from the comments of Jesus to the offering of the widow, the so-called widow's mite. While many people were putting money into the collection box[28] from the abundance of their wealth, this widow offered her last two coins (Mk 12:42f).[29] Her offering did not escape the notice of Jesus. This sort of whole-hearted giving is what Jesus recommends to his followers. At least this is the traditional understanding of this passage.[30] And if the poor widow were to use her last two lepta to support her parents rather than offer them to God it is to be assumed that she would have received even more praise from Jesus (cf. Mk 7:10-13).[31] But it is not uncommon to hear Christians

---

[27] H. Lansdell, Sacred Tenth, 1:158.

[28] This collection box had the form of a trumpet. The little opening for casting in the offering is meant to prevent stealing from it. The difficulty for anybody sitting opposite this collection box to see what is put inside has made some scholars to suggest that what Jesus narrated was a parable that has been given a historical garb. See E. Haenchen, Der Weg, 432f.

[29] For a wide range of scholarly opinions on this passage see A. G. Wright, "The Widow's Mites: Praise or Lament?—A Matter of Context," CBQ 44 (1982), 256-265.

[30] It is interesting the conclusion Wright arrives at in his study of this pericope. He links the passage of the 'widow's mite' with the condemnation of the scribes who devour widow's houses and as pretense make long prayers (Mk 12:38-40). This widow who had only two small coins left was forced by her religious thinking to offer the last thing she had to the very people who had devoured her belongings. In the mind of Wright, the words of Jesus were not an approbation but a condemnation of this religious system. A. G. Wright, "The Widow's Mites," CBQ 44 (1982), 261-263. Wright is not alone in this argument. For Fleddermann, the house of the widow in our passage has been devoured by her gifts to the Temple treasury. See H. Fleddermann, "A Warning about the Scribes (Mk 12.37b-40)," CBQ44 (1982), 61-67. See also Q Quesnell, "The Mind of Mark Interpretation and Method through the Exegesis of Mark 6,52" AnBib 38, Rome Biblical Institute, (1969) 151. But no matter how this passage is interpreted, this widow is to be seen in a better light than those for whose benefit she made this offering.

[31] For a discussion of the various aspects of Corban, see K. H. Rengstorf, "Korban" TDNT Vol. III. 860-866; J. A. Fitzmyer, "The Aramaic Qorbän Inscription from Jebel

who challenge God and remind him of the necessity of doing something for them based on their ability to pay their tithes. If the widow is to be an example for the followers of Jesus, then she paid more than a tenth of her possession and probably did not hold God to ransom because of this.

But for those who pay their tithe and regard it as their right to receive blessings from God based on this, there is also a biblical companion. The only problem is that this companion of theirs is a Pharisee, one of the most avowed opponents of Jesus. In his prayer in the Temple, the Pharisee stood and prayed thus with himself, "God, I thank thee that I am not like other men, extortioners, unjust, adulterers, or even like this tax collector. I fast twice a week, I give tithes of all that I get" (Lk 18:11f). He had a nice CV and PR, yet he was not recommended by Jesus. This shows that there is a more important criterion of credibility before God than tithing.

As already shown, the Mishna bears witnesses that tithe-paying was current during the years after Jesus of Nazareth. This is also evident from what Josephus (Born 37 AD) said about the High Priest Annas:

> "He also had servants who were very wicked, who joined themselves to the boldest sort of the people, and went to the threshing- floors and took away the tithes that belonged to the priests, by violence, and did not refrain from beating such as would not give these tithes to them. So also other High Priests acted in the like manner, as did those his servants, without any one's being able to prohibit them: so that some of the priests that of old were wont to be supported with those tithes died for want of food."[32]

Hallet et-Turi and Mk 7:11/Mt 15:5," Essays on the Semitic Background of the New Testament (London, 1971), 93-100.

[32] Josephus, Ant. Bk XX, Ch. IX, sect IX.

About his own handling of the tithe Josephus makes the following comments:

> "As to what presents were offered to me, I despised them, as not standing in need of them; nor indeed would I take the tithes which were due to me as a priest, from those that brought them."[33]

Josephus is here alluding to the tithe that was legally his as a priest.[34] This means that the payment of tithe was current in his days. We have already seen the limited nature of the tithe paid to the priests. The Levites were the main recipients of OT tithe.

Despite this continued offering of the tithe, Jesus enjoined his followers to a better form of giving. His teaching centered on the sort of offering that comes from the heart. This is the kind of offering that his early followers also pursued.

5.4 The Early Christians and Tithing

Having gone through the teachings of Jesus with regard to the Jewish Law in general and to tithing in particular, it is evident that Jesus encouraged the act of generosity in giving and in receiving. He also did not repeal the Torah's teaching on tithes.[35] On the other hand, he never made tithing the central tenet of his teaching. Rather, he considered justice, faith and mercy heavier issues than tithe. If these teachings are taken to be from the historical Jesus, then they were rendered during the second Temple period with an active Temple cult involving the presence of the official Jewish priesthood and Levites. It must be important to note the way his earlier followers continued on this principle after him and especially after the destruction of the Temple and the dissolution of the Jewish priesthood and ritual offering.

---

[33] Josephus, Life, sect XV.

[34] He was a descendant of the High Priest Jonathan. See F. Millar, History, 45-46.

[35] We have argued elsewhere that the community of Matthew may have continued with the practice of tithing. See R. Onyenali, Trilogy, 243.

The early Christians seem not to have paid attention to any tithing of any sort. Scarcely had Peter finished his Pentecost preaching than we read that the whole community was united in heart and in spirit and everyone shared everything in common. The result was that there was not a needy person among them, for as many as were possessors of lands or houses sold them, and brought the proceeds of what was sold and laid it at the apostles' feet; and distribution was made to each as any had need. (Acts 4:34f). Here, the early followers of Jesus have already surpassed the tithe and have started giving all they had in accordance with the teachings of Jesus. One of those to perform this noble act was Barnabas whose generosity earned him the name 'the son of encouragement' (Acts 4:36). The negative folio was the family of Ananias and Sapphira who brought a portion of the proceeds from what they sold and pretended to have brought the whole (Acts 5:1). Later, we learn that there was a church provision meant for taking care of the poor. This is shown by the murmuring of the Hellenists over the neglect of their poor (Acts 6:1). This led to the institution of the diaconate (Acts 7:1-3). Later on we read that there were Jewish converts to Christianity who still observed the Law (Acts 21:20). But we are not told that they paid the tenth of their possession. For Lansdell, tithing should be seen as part of observing the Law.[36] But one wonders what kind of need tithing would solve with new arrangement of the community as noted above.

If we turn to the regions outside Palestine, we recall a number of the early characters in the Christian writings depicted as serving examples of alms giving in the post-70 AD years. We know of Tabitha (Acts 9:36-39) and Cornelius (Acts 10: 1-5). The argument that Peter was a faithful tithe-payer is followed by Lansdell[37] which he argues was very

---

[36] H. Lansdell, Sacred Tenth, 1:165. One could comfortably conclude that Lansdell pressed out of every mention of obedience to the Law in the bible to point to obedience to paying the tithe. This is a perfect example of trying hard to press out titheable theological juice from every passage of the bible.

[37] Cf. H. Lansdell, Sacred Tenth, 1:263f.

prominent at that time. His argument is based on the fact that nowhere in the Acts of the Apostles was tithe repealed or rescinded. But this argument from silence cannot be considered convincing.

The evidence we get from the writings of the New Testament lead to the conclusion that the teaching of tithing was not prominent despite the great premium placed on alms giving. Tithing has been replaced by the communal life of the early believers. However, it should be assumed that the practice of having everything in common did not continue for a long time. It is possible that this exercise of having everything in common was limited to the church in Jerusalem. One of the problems Paul addressed among the faithful in Corinth concerned a situation whereby some had more than abundance while others did not have enough (cf. 1Cor 11.20f). So, the experience of the church of Jerusalem may have become obsolete for the church in Corinth only after few years. It also happened that Paul had the need of helping the needy in some of the churches he got into contact with. In the early days of his ministry in Antioch, during the reign of Tiberius Claudius Nero Germanicus (41-54),[38] a certain prophet named Agabus came from Jerusalem to Antioch and prophesied the advent of a great famine (cf. Acts 11:27f). This made the disciples to determine, *everyone according to his ability*, to send relief to Judea. Surely there is no idea of tithing in the mind of the disciples. In his endeavour to get the most out of his rich and philanthropic congregation in Corinth, Paul propounded a teaching on which many Christians have based to build a New Testament theology of giving. Following the natural laws of agriculture, Paul says, "he who sows sparingly will also reap sparingly, and he who sows bountifully will also reap bountifully. Each one must do *as he has made up his mind, not reluctantly or under compulsion,* for God loves a

---

[38] From secular history we learn that the reign of Claudius witnessed series of droughts. Cf. Suetonius, Claudius 18.2. There could be a reference to this in Josephus, Ant. iii. 320; xx. 51 ff., 101. The fate of Christianity under Claudius has been studied by F. F. Bruce, "Christianity Under Claudius," BJRL 44 (March 1962): 309-326.

cheerful giver" (2 Cor 9:6f). The idea of free donation is again commended in this passage. It should also be noted that the donation in vogue here was not for the apostle himself but for the poor. He made it clear that he worked to earn his living: "to the present hour we hunger and thirst, we are ill-clad and buffeted and homeless, and we labour, working with our own hands" (1 Cor 4:11f). This does not preclude the fact that some other disciples enjoyed some form of assistance from their congregations (cf. 1 Cor 9:1-18). The above text sees the apostle Paul employ the authority of the Lord to declare that those who preach the gospel should live by the gospel (1 Cor 9:14). That the labourer deserves his wages is only but normal. From where do we expect our spiritual leaders to earn their living if not from what we give them? So Paul laboured for his own subsistence while collecting free will donations for the poor mother church in Jerusalem.

But even if the early followers of Jesus did or did not offer tithe (our conclusion is that they did not), there is another aspect of NT theology that could be decisive in the appreciation of the current practice of the priesthood of believers. We turn to the letter to the Hebrews for this developed view of the priesthood. This is important since it is argued in many quarters that Christians should offer the tithe for the upkeep of the priests of their various churches.

5.5 The Priesthood of Christ and the Priesthood of Melchizedek (Heb 7:4-20)

Although the seventh chapter of the letter to the Hebrews was not the first place that the author introduced the priesthood of Christ, it is in this chapter that the notion is given a well thought-out exposition. The sixth chapter already concluded by stating that Jesus is a priest forever according to the order of Melchizedek (6:20). As W. L. Lane points out, "the clear allusion to Ps 110:4 in the description of Christ as the heavenly high priest in 6:20 sets the stage for the midrash that follows."[39]

In fact, the employment of the midrash forms a constitutive element of the letter to the Hebrews.[40] The dominant OT texts are Gen 14:17-20 and Ps 110:4. The seventh chapter of Hebrews is very important for our case because it is the only post-Easter NT mention of tithing.[41] While "tithe/tenth" is found in Heb 7:2.4.5.6.8.9, there is no mention of tithe or giving the tenth part again in the NT post Easter. The connection between the priesthood and tithe in this chapter makes it indispensable for any NT treatise on tithing. Let us look at the way Christ and Melchizedek are connected in the priestly treaties of the letter.

In this chapter, the author tells us that Melchizedek was the king of Salem and the priest of the Most High God (7:1). Here his priestly and kingly status comes to the fore. The letter recounts the gift of Abraham to Melchizedek (7:2). Melchizedek's greatness is shown by Abraham paying a tithe to him (7:6). Since the lesser is blessed by the greater, Melchizedek blessed Abraham, thus showing again his greatness (7:7). Already one sees how the letter has reversed the chronology of blessing and tithing. While the Melchizedek pericope tells us that the blessing of Melchizedek preceded the gift of Abram (Gen 14:18-20), the letter to the Hebrews implies that Abram's gift came before the blessing.[42] A second problem is the fact that for one to be a Levitical priest he must trace his descent to the line of Aaron. Failure to produce such a pedigree automatically debars one from being recognized as a priest. When the Jews returned from the exile in Babylon certain families from the tribe

---

[39] W. L. Lane, Hebrews 1-8 (WBC 47a), 158.

[40] The midrash can simply be explained as a form of biblical interpretation based on the supposition that if different passages of the scripture contain the same words, the verbal correspondence is enough reason for interpreting one text in the light of the other. This method is seen again in 1:5; 3:7-4:11; 13:5-6).

[41] This is based on the assumption that the synoptic references to tithe reflect the words of the historical Jesus.

[42] But one can also discover a balanced structural symmetry between vv 1-3 and vv 4-10. While in vv 1-3 we see: the meeting (v 1a), the blessing (v 1b) and the tithe (v 2), in vv 4-10 we see: the tithe (v 4), the blessing (v 6) and the meeting (v 10). This point has already been made by W. L. Lane, Hebrews, 159f.

of Levi could not produce their genealogical records. This made them to be excluded from the priestly office (Ezra 2:61-63; Neh 7:63-65). But instead of arguing that Jesus was not a priest since he comes from the tribe of Judah, the author concludes that Jesus comes from the priestly order of Melchizedek, a priestly order not based on descent but on the will of God, a priesthood not based on inheritance but personal character. This means that he is greater than Abraham. Therefore, he is also greater than the Levitical priests who were in the bosom of Abraham when he paid tithes to Melchizedek (7:10).[43] A third problem is that while Gen 14:17 tells us that it was the king of Sodom that met Abram, Heb 7:1 tells us that Abram was met by Melchizedek. This idea is repeated in 7:10.[44]

The presentation of Melchizedek in the letter to the Hebrews resembles the idea of the priest king in Ancient Near East which we have already discussed. Lack of knowledge of his genealogy (7:3a)[45] makes him akin to the sacral kings already seen in the Ancient Near East. This is made explicit in vv.1-3. Although the kingly status of Melchizedek features more in the letter, his priestly component cannot be overlooked. Apart from this chapter, his priestly function is scattered in many passages of the letter (cf. 1:3; 3:1-6; 4:14; 5:5-6.10; 10:12-13.21). This section would study Heb 7:4-20 in two sub-sections: 7:4-10 and 7:11-20.

---

[43] According to Horton, the author of Hebrews selected Melchizedek to be the model was because "Melchizedek is the first priest mentioned in the Torah". F. L. Horton, Melchizedek Traditions, 157.

[44] W. L. Lane has seen the beautiful inclusio formed in these two verses by the repeated statement that Melchizedek met Abraham. Hebrews, 159.

[45] The absence of information about the background of Melchizedek informs the statement that nothing is known of his origin. This underscores the fact that in midrash, the silence of scripture is charged with significance

5.5.1 The Priesthood of Melchizedek and the Tithe of Abraham (Heb 7:4-10)

We have already seen the kingly (→2.4) and priestly (→2.5) status of Melchizedek. This section investigates one of the earliest Christian exegeses on this encounter between Abram and Melchizedek.

> Just see how great this man was--Abraham gave him the tenth of the spoils of victory--and Abraham was no less than the founder of our nation. Now look at the difference--when the sons of Levi receive their priesthood, they receive an injunction laid down by the law to exact tithes from the people. That is to say, they exact tithes from their own brothers, even though they are descendants of Abraham. But this man, whose descent is not traced through them at all, exacted tithes from Abraham and actually blessed the man who had received the promises. Beyond all argument the lesser is blessed by the greater. Just so, in the one instance, it is the case of men who die receiving tithes; but in this instance, it is the case of a man whom the evidence proves to live. Still further, if I may put it this way, through Abraham Levi, too, the very man who receives the tithes, had tithes exacted from him, for he was in his father's body when Melchizedek met him.

The first notable point is that the author of our text treats the encounter between Abram and Melchizedek as a historic event. Although this passage makes numerous references to tithe, the primary concern is to show the superiority of the priesthood of Christ over the Levitical priesthood.[46] It draws heavily from Numbers 18, which established the principle of tithing. William Barclay has isolated the main outline of the

---

[46] For L. Kim, the rhetoric in Hebrews 7 is anti-Jewish polemic for the purpose of legitimizing Jesus' priesthood over against the Levitical and subverting allegiance to the dominant Jewish society. See his Polemic in the book of Hebrews, 96.

arguments of the above passage.[47] We have also added some points to his insights. (i) The Levites receive tithes from the people and that is a right that only they enjoy. Although Melchizedek was not a Levite yet he received tithe from Abraham. (ii) The Levites tithe their brother Israelites; Melchizedek was not an Israelite but a stranger; and it was no ordinary Israelite from whom he received tithes but from no less a person than Abraham, the founder of the nation.[48] (iii) It was due to a legal enactment that the Levites have the right to exact tithes. This means the tithing cannot be separated from the commandment of the law which gave rise to the institution of the Levitical priesthood (7:5). But Melchizedek received tithes for the sake of what he was personally. He had such personal greatness that he needed no legal enactment to entitle him to receive tithes. (iv) In each of the four evidences in 7:4-10, tithing is used to prove that Christ's priesthood is superior to that of the Levites. (v) The Levites receive tithes as dying men; but Melchizedek lives forever. (vi) Finally the author produces a curious argument for which he apologizes before he states it: Levi was a direct descendant of Abraham and the only man legally entitled to receive tithes. Now, if he was a direct descendant of Abraham it means that he was already in Abraham's body. This informs the description of Abraham as patriarch. This means that "Abraham is not simply an individual, but a representative figure in this context."[49] Therefore when Abraham paid tithes to Melchizedek, Levi also paid them, being included in Abraham's body, the final proof that Melchizedek was superior to him.

In the main, the passage contrasts the mortal Aaronic priesthood, which was partially sustained by tithing principles, with Christ's priesthood according to the order of Melchizedek. This new priesthood is eternal and sustained by God's grace. This implies that there is a

---

[47] W. Barclay, Hebrews, 76.

[48] In Heb 7:4 Abraham was exalted only to emphasize the exalted status of Melchizedek even more. W. L. Lane, Hebrews, 168.

[49] W. L. Lane, Hebrews, 168.

change in the priestly order and guiding principles. This is what the next pericope in the letter addresses.

5.5.2 Change in the Priestly Order and Change in Tithing Principles (Heb 7:11-20)

The foregoing discussions have shown that the Levitical priestly order was not able to achieve the required result. This called for the need for a new priestly order.

> If, then, the desired effect could have been achieved by the Levitical priesthood--for it was on the basis of it that the people became a people of the law--what further need was there to set up another priest, and to call him a priest after the order of Melchizedek, and not to call him a priest after the order of Aaron? Once the priesthood was altered, of necessity there follows an alteration of the law, too, for the person of whom the statements are made belongs to another tribe altogether, from which no one ever served at the altar. It is obvious that it was from Judah that our Lord sprang, and with regard to that tribe Moses said nothing about priests. And certain things are still more abundantly clear--if a different priest is set up, a priest after the order of Melchizedek, a priest who has become so, not according to the law of a mere human injunction but according to the power of life that is indestructible--for the witness of scripture in regard to this is: 'You are a priest for ever after the order of Melchizedek'--if all that is so, two things emerge. On the one hand, there emerges the cancellation of the previous injunction because of its own weakness and uselessness (for the law never achieved the effect it was designed to produce) and, on the other hand, there emerges the introduction of a better hope through which we can come near to God.

We feel that the above passage summarizes the whole argument on the enduring role of the sons of Aaron with regard to their rights and responsibilities. Since their function has been abrogated by the enduring priesthood of Christ, it also follows that their benefits no longer have any relevance. The old law has been cancelled with all its legislations. The word used for cancellation is the Greek athetesis, that is, the word used for annulling a treaty, for abrogating a promise, for scoring a man's name off the register, for rendering a law or regulation inoperative. The whole paraphernalia of the ceremonial law was wiped out in the priesthood of Jesus.[50] As L. Kim concluded, "what is clear from the argument is that there can be only one priesthood in the Jewish religious system. Because of this presupposition, once the final, more superior priesthood came, the former priesthood and law no longer had any use."[51]

This type of explanation has followed the long history of biblical interpretation of this passage in the church. As early as the fourth century Chrysostom made the following comments:

By saying "according to the order of Melchizedek" [Heb. 7:11], he expels (ἐξέβαλεν) the order of Aaron ... He became a priest, he says, not according to the law of a carnal commandment (σαρκικῆς ἐντολῆς) [Heb. 7:16], for in many ways that law was really no law (ἄνομος), and he spoke well when he called it a carnal commandment, for all things were limited to the carnal (σαρκικά), as it says, circumcise the flesh (σάρκα), anoint the flesh, wash the flesh, purify the flesh, shave the flesh, fasten on the flesh, take care of the flesh, laze in the flesh ... He says that "the previous commandment has been set aside (ἀθέτησις), because it was weak (ἀσθενές) and ineffective (ἀνωφελές)" [Heb.

---

[50] W. Barclay, Hebrews, 79.

[51] L. Kim, Polemic in the Book of Hebrews, 93. However, this sort of argument seems to neglect the fact that the priesthood of Melchizedek preceded the Levitical priesthood. If the priesthood of Melchizedek was superior why did God institute the priesthood of the Levites?

7:18] ...What is this "setting aside"? A substitution (ἄμειψις), and a throwing-away (ἐκβολή) ... for the law perfected nothing, all were types, everything was a shadow, be it circumcision, sacrifice, or Sabbath.[52]

The anti-Semitic tone of these lines cannot be overlooked. Not only are the laws of Aaron expelled, they are called a carnal commandment. The reason for setting aside this carnal law was because of its ineffectiveness to effect the desired result.

With regard to our topic of discussion, the main lines of argument from this pericope could be summarized in the following points: (i) The Old Covenant methods of worshiping God through the Mosaic priesthood involving tithes, offerings and sacrifices have failed (7:11). (ii) This failure of the old covenant implied the need for a new system of approaching God (7:11). (iii) The change of the old covenant with its priesthood involves a replacement or suppression of the old principles (7:12). (iv) Since Christ came from Judah and not from Levi, it is evident that he could not collect the tithe that was meant for the Levitical priests (7:13-14). (v) Also because Christ's priesthood does not derive from the Levitical priesthood, nothing in the law concerning the priesthood of the old covenant should be applied to him (7:15). (vi) The priesthood of Melchizedek and of Christ are not governed by any human laws but by the power of God (7:16-17). (vii) The reason for setting aside the old law was because it was weak and ineffective (7:18). (viii) It is only through the application of the new principles of hope that humans can achieve spiritual perfection (7:19). (ix) The priesthood of the sons of Aaron has been replaced by the priesthood of all believers (7:19).

---

[52] John Chrysostom, Homily 13; PG 63, 103-105. For analysis of Chrysostom's commentary see J. A. Barnard, "Anti-Jewish Interpretations of Hebrews: Some Neglected Factors," Melilah, Vol. 11 (2014), 37f.

We thus see a lot of contrast between the Levitical priesthood and the priesthood of the new dispensation. Since the old priesthood has been dissolved it becomes irrelevant to point to the tenets of the old law as justification for the actions of the new law. This is made explicit in 7:12. This verse states that when there is a change of the priesthood there should be a corresponding change in the law. The survey we made on the OT tithe seems to be dissolving before our eyes. This is because there is no atom of doubt that the priesthood has changed. This is the lesson we get from the letter to the Hebrews and also from the existential experiences of modern-day priesthood in the Christian religion. If we take the Catholic Church as typical example because of her continued use of the priest terminology, there is no way one could compare her priesthood with the Levitical priesthood without arriving at enormous differences. The clergy of the other Christian denominations are even far removed from this schema. However, the question remains whether there is a corresponding change in the law of tithing from the Church.

But one could also argue that the recourse to the priesthood of Melchizedek is a justification for the enduring relevance of tithing since Melchizedek accepted tithe from Abraham. This is a plausible suggestion. But does it not involve reading into the text? The fact that Jesus did not receive tithe and did not make preaching the tithe the hallmark of his ministry shows that this law is already superseded. We have already seen how his earlier followers catered for their needs through generous donation from the wealthy in their midst.

5.6 Summary of Findings

Our long excursus in this chapter has shown that Jesus did not do away with the Mosaic Law per se. In many instances he refined the precepts of this law and argued strongly against the traditions of the elders that relegate the laws of God to the background. The mind of Jesus was to call his audience to the original spirit of the law of God given through Moses. But when we come to the area of the tithe, the only reference Jesus made was to admonish the scribes not to neglect the heavier matters of the law in pursuit of paying tithes of herbs and food seasoners. Rather, he encouraged generous giving. This teaching was carried forth in the examples of the communities of the early Christians and in the letters of Paul. It is clear from the evidence of the NT that the early Christians neither taught nor practiced tithing. To give joyfully according to the ability of the giver was the underlining principle.

But there is a book of the NT that makes special reference to tithe: the letter to the Hebrews. We are witnesses to how this letter effectively dissolved the threads that were supposed to bind the priesthood of the new era to the priesthood of Aaron. In this letter, the example of Abram is recalled to show his payment of tithe to Melchizedek. It is assumed that since the priesthood of Christ is according to the order of Melchizedek, Christian priests are entitled to receive tithes from those they bless. But this letter makes a clarion call in 7:12 that the law should be changed if there is a change in the priesthood. This call has summarized our efforts in this chapter. Definitely the priesthood has changed. This change was already seen by the early church. The next chapter leads us to an encounter of tithing during the post-apostolic time.

CHAPTER SIX

TITHING IN THE POST-APOSTOLIC CHURCH

Having reached thus far in our study of the principle of tithing from the OT to the NT, one has the feeling that the study is already cruising home. But as R. T. Kendal said, "the definitive statement on [tithing] has yet to be written."[1] In fact, any statement about tithing must look at the prevailing economic and cultic circumstances of the religion in question. The previous chapters have shown us that an exclusive dependence on the dictates of the OT may not do justice to the new covenant inaugurated in the person of Jesus. This means that the followers of the law of grace have the freedom to enact rules to guide their relationship with God under the guidance of the Holy Spirit. Let us see how the post-apostolic church reacted to this new situation with regard to the payment of tithes. We begin with the document of the ancient church called the Didache.

6. 1 The Didache

One of the most recent studies on the Didache is the 2015 publication of Draper et al.[2] The study makes it evident to the reader how important this document of the early church has been to scholars since its discovery less than 150 years ago. Despite this short span of life, it has generated a disproportionate interest from Christian theologians.[3] In his own contribution, Milavec avers that in as much as the book of the Acts

---

[1] R. T. Kendall, Tithing, 43.

[2] J. A. Draper/C. N. Jefford, The Didache: A Missing Piece of the Puzzle in Early Christianity. Atlanta, 2015. Among the more useful studies of the Didache, the following stand out: F. E. Volkes, The Riddle of the Didache: Fact or Fiction, Heresy or Catholicism? London, 1938; C. N. Jefford, The Teaching of the Twelve Apsotles: Didache. Santa Rosa, 2013; A. Milavec, The Didache: Text, Translation, Analysis and Commentary. Minnesota, 2003.

[3] J. A. Draper, C. N. Jefford, The Didache, 1.

of the Apostles gives insight into some historical events in the life of the Church and while the letters of St Paul offer occasional windows into the life of the communities he founded, the Didache offers a full-blown description of nearly every aspect of community life among the early Christians.[4] This short book is placed by scholars around the middle to the end of the first century AD and is considered a genuine document of the early church.

In a passage in the Didache we read the following: "...But whoever says in the Spirit, Give me money, or something else, you shall not listen to him. But if he tells you to give for others' sake who are in need, let no one judge him."[5] What makes this citation significant is that it comes in the context of discernment of spirit. The document recommends that anyone who speaks in spirit should not be judged. However, it gives the markers of a false prophet, namely, if he asks for money for himself, if he asks for bread and eats it, and any prophet who does not practice what he preaches. With this small notice, the document seems to continue the tradition attributed to Jesus by the canonical writers (cf. Mt 23:2). The main concern of a genuine prophet is not the material wellbeing of the prophet or missionary but the care of those in need. This gives modern Christians a further criterion for the discernment of true and false prophets: any prophet that asks for money is a false prophet. Just like the writings of the NT canon show, the issue of charity was important for the composers of the Didache.[6]

Luckily for us, we also read from the Didache pointers to the problem posed by the OT demand of tithe. In a passage we read:

---

[4] A. Milavec, The Didache, x.

[5] Chapter 11. Concerning Teachers, Apostles, and Prophets. See W. North, The Didache, 11.

[6] The Didache discusses other forms of charity. In 1:6 the early Christians were encouraged to let their charitable gifts sweat in their hands until they know to whom they were giving it. See also 4:8 that talks about the communal living of Christians.

"No more be bound with sin offerings, holocausts, etc., nor yet with tithes and first fruits, and part-offerings, and gifts and oblations. For it was laid upon them to give all these things as of necessity, but you are not bound by these things...thus shall your righteousness abound more than their tithes and first fruits and part-offerings, when you shall do it as it is written: 'Sell all thou hast, and give it to the poor'"[7]

The above citation is curious because the early church prophets were wandering preachers who had to move from community to community to spread the message of their Lord. It would have been consistent with the Jewish teaching to render a tenth of the believers' increase of land and flock for the support of such itinerant teachers. It becomes more curious when one sees that the Didache identifies these prophets as "the High Priests" of the Christian communities.[8] This brings them closer to the Levites of the old law. Rather, what the Didache allows to be given to the High Priests of the new dispensation is the gift of the first fruits.[9] With the early church identifying her prophets as priests, one already sees some difficulty in making a combination of the teachings of the Old and New testaments. "Nothing in the many varieties of Judaism suggests the substitution of the prophet for the high priest, just as nothing in the Christian Scriptures prepares one literally to offer first fruits."[10] There is also an apparent problem when the Didache enjoins believers to give as they think best and to give according to the commandment (13:4). What commandment is being referred to here? This could be seen as a contradiction if the commandment is a reference to the OT.[11] To avoid

---

[7] Didache, 2.35.
[8] See chapter 13 on the support of the prophets. For further analysis see A. Milavec, The Didache, 498.
[9] Didache 13:3.
[10] A. Milavec, The Didache, 494.
[11] This is the conclusion of T. J. Powers, Historical Study of the Tithe, 16.

this apparent contradiction one has to see the commandment as referring to the principle already enunciated by the Teacher.[12] The commandment is the argument against the presentation sin offerings, holocausts, tithes, first fruits, etc. It appears that what is at stake here is a pastoral approach to the current issues of the reflecting community based on their understanding of salvation history and the support of the clergy. This process would be carried forth during the time of the second century Christians and their immediate followers.

6.2 Tithe in the Second Century Church

The Christians of the second century could rightly be called the second fruits of the apostolic ministry. Perhaps the first prominent person to leave an extant teaching or mention of tithe during this time is Justin the Martyr (AD 100-AD 165). In his first Apology[13] he gives insight into the Christian liturgy. He tells us that Christians gather on the day called Sunday to read the memoirs of the apostles or the writings of the prophets. These are followed by instructions from the president of the assembly, prayers and sharing the love meal. Afterwards, "they who are well to do, and willing, give what each thinks fit; and what is collected is deposited with the president, who succors the orphans and widows and those who, through sickness or any other cause, are in want, and those who are in bonds and the strangers sojourning among us, and in a word takes care of all who are in need."[14] But after this first offering they took a second offering for the clergy. One easily sees from the citation above that the stress of Justin is the element of free will donation. Again, this donation is mainly expected to come from the rich members of the community. This means that he did not advocate tithing.[15]

---

[12] This is the approach adopted by D. A. Croteau, You Mean I Don't Have to Tithe, 11.

[13] Justin, First Apology, Ch. LXVII.

[14] Justin, First Apology, Ch. LXVII.

[15] This conclusion is also arrived at by D. A. Croteau, You Mean I Don't Have to Tithe, 12.

The above conclusion is to be expected from Justin who is to be seen as one of the strongest apologists of the Christian movement against Judaism. This is well seen in his Dialogue with Trypho, the Jew. In this Dialogue, Justin makes two statements which could represent a summary of his notion of the Jewish law. In the first statement he says: "But we do not trust through Moses or through the law; for then we would do the same as yourselves." In the second statement we read: "Now, law placed against law has abrogated that which is before it, and a covenant which comes after in like manner has put an end to the previous one; and an eternal and final law—namely, Christ —has been given to us, and the covenant is trustworthy, after which there shall be no law, no commandment, no ordinance."[16] This argument resembles the repudiation of the Levitical priesthood already contained in the letter to the Hebrews. Even if tithing was in vogue during the time of Justin, the above remarks show that he could have repudiated it based on his strong aversion to the Jewish law.

Another Christian apologist, Irenaeus (AD 130- AD 200) follows the same trend of argument as Justin. In his Adversus Hereseus, he provides an ancient treatise of the relationship between the law and the gospel. With regard to the offertory of Christians he says concerning the plans of God: "For with Him there is nothing purposeless, nor without signification, nor without design. And for this reason they (the Jews) had indeed the tithes of their goods consecrated to Him, but those who have received liberty set aside all their possessions for the Lord's purposes, bestowing joyfully and freely not the less valuable portions of their property, since they have the hope of better things [hereafter]; as that poor widow acted who cast all her living into the treasury of God"[17] We are already in a situation where the words of Jesus in the gospels and the actions of the disciples are echoed in the teaching of this second century

---

[16] Justin, Dialogue XI.
[17] Irenaeus, Against Heresies, book 4, chap. 18.

Bishop. To show that this kind of giving is deeper than the law of Moses recommended, Irenaeus goes on to say: "And for this reason did the Lord, instead of that [commandment], 'You shall not commit adultery,' forbid even concupiscence; and instead of that which runs thus, 'You shall not kill,' He prohibited anger; and instead of the law enjoining the giving of tithes, to share all our possessions with the poor…"[18] Finally, Irenaeus tells us what is obligatory for Christians, and that is, "we are bound…to offer God the first fruit of his creation."[19] One could then conclude that "the whole spirit of Irenaeus was that the law of the tithe has been abrogated."[20]

Another ancient father to be considered in this study is Clement of Alexandria (AD 153- AD 217). In his Stromata, which is the third of his trilogy of writings on the Christian life, he teaches the importance of the Mosaic Law in teaching piety, justice, faith and love among other virtues. In chapter two of this writing, Clement places tithing in the same category as the Sabbatical Year and the year of Jubilee, arguing that they are not compulsory for Christians but should be done for the spiritual well-being of the giver.[21] Some commentators have used this piece of information to argue that Clement advocated tithe[22] but it is easy to see that his conclusion is that those who teach tithes should also teach the importance of the Sabbatical and Jubilee years. In chapter eighteen of book two, he sees the Mosaic Law as the fountain of all ethics, and the source from which the Greeks drew theirs. For him, the tithes of the first fruits and of the flocks taught both piety towards the Deity, and not covetously to grasp everything, but to gifts of kindness to ones neighbour. He reckons that it was from the first fruits that the priests were maintained.[23]

---

18 Cf. R. E. Kelly, A Secular History of Tithing, 253-254.
19 Cf. D. A. Croteau, You Mean I Don't have to Tithe, 12f.
20 T. J. Powers, Historical Study of the Tithe, 21.
21 Clement of Alexandria, Stromata, 2.18.
22 See for instance A. V. Babbs, Law of the Tithe, 112.

His most eminent student, Origen takes up this teaching in his eleventh commentary on the book of Numbers chapter 18. Part of his teaching is that "it is good and profitable that first fruits be offered to (or 'for') the priests of the gospel also, for so also hath the Lord ordained, that they who preach the gospel should live of the gospel, and that those who wait at the altar should participate from the altar. And as this is worthy and decent, so, on the contrary, I think it indecent, unworthy and impious, that he who worships God, and enters the house of God, who knows that priests and ministers wait at the altar…should not offer to the priests the first fruits of the fruits which God gives by making the sun to shine and the rain to fall."[24] With reference to Luke 11:42 Origen maintains that the greater things of the law as well as the lesser things of the law should be observed. However, Origen seems to imply that the followers of Jesus should give more than the requirements of the law. This is so since the life of the Christian is a call to greater righteousness than that of the Pharisees (Mt 5:20).

There are numerous other studies that have surveyed the development of tithe in the later history of the church. The conclusion drawn by majority of these sources is that it was not practiced in the early Christian church until the 6th century. We therefore summarize this section with the statement from the Catholic Encyclopedia (1912 edition):

"in the beginning [provision] was supplied by the spontaneous support of the faithful. In the course of time, however, as the church expanded and various institutions arose, it became necessary to make laws which will ensure the proper and permanent support of the clergy. The payment of tithes was adopted from the Old Law and early writers speak of it as a divine ordinance and an obligation of the conscience. The earliest

---

[23] Clement of Alexandria, Stromata, Bk II, Ch.18.
[24] Quoted in H. Lansdell, Sacred Tenth, 1:182.

positive legislation on the subject seems to be contained in the letter of the bishops at Tours in 567 and the Canons of the Council of Marcon in 585."[25]

Despite strong arguments that favour this conclusion, there is still the presence of some ancient and modern sources that claim that tithing has gone uninterrupted throughout the history of the church.[26] Such theses are difficult to sustain.

It seems as though the rise and fall of tithing in the church is intrinsically linked with the rise and fall of tithing in Europe. The implication is that one finds it difficult to discuss the tithe as a form of religious tax unconnected with obligation to the state. This is because of the fusion between church and state shortly after Christianity became state religion from the fifth century. Most of the available records of laws regarding tithes come from England and show how the history of tithing has endured tremendous changes. As the records show, tithing became law in England as far back as the ninth century, and still existed ten years later. But because of the industrialization of the nineteenth century, coupled with religious dissent and agricultural depression, tithe became unattractive for tithe payers.[27] Those mostly infuriated by the payment of the tithe were the farmers since manufactured goods were not subject to tithes. In England in the 10th century, payment of tithe was made obligatory under ecclesiastical penalties by Edmund I and under temporal penalties by

---

[25] The Catholic Encyclopedia, Vol. XIV (1912), s.v. "Tithe." See also R. E. Kelly, Conclusion, 260.

[26] During the course of this research we stumbled across the work of T. Comber on the Historic vindication of the divine right of tithes. In chapter four of his work, he examined tithe within the first four hundred years after Christ. His conclusion is that Christ did not discourage but rather encouraged the act of tithing. This teaching was carried on by the early Christians in the persons of Clement of Alexandria, Origen, Jerome, etc. His work published in 1682 was designed to supply the omissions, answer the objections, and rectify the mistakes of J. Selden's History of Tithes published in 1618. For his work, Selden was summoned before king James to answer for the issues raised. He was made to apologize to the high commission of bishops and forbidden to reply to the commissioned attacks against him. Comber's work seems to be one of the commissioned attacks against Selden. It makes some conclusions that cannot be supported using the methods of either ancient or modern exegesis.

[27] See W. Foot et al, Maps for Family and Local History: The Records of the Tithe, Valuation, 13.

Edgar. In the 14th century Pope Gregory VII, in an effort to control abuses, outlawed lay ownership of tithes. During the 16th-century Protestant Reformation, Martin Luther approved in general paying of tithes to the temporal sovereign, and the imposition of tithes continued for the benefit of Protestant as well as Roman Catholic churches. Gradually, however, opposition grew. Tithes were repealed in France during the Revolution (1789), without compensation to tithe holders. Other countries abolished certain kinds of tithes and indemnified the holders. By 1887 the tithe had been brought to an end in Italy. It was abolished in Ireland at the disestablishment of the Anglican church in 1871, and it gradually died out in the Church of Scotland.[28]

Numerous church councils have debated the importance of tithes in particular and the welfare of the clergy of the church in general. But we will consider the Councils of Tours, Trent and Vatican II because of their importance in shaping the history and theology of the Church.

6.3 Tithe and Church Councils

As the conclusion of the previous section shows, both the earliest Christian writers as well as the first councils of the church seemed not positively disposed to adopting the Jewish law of tithe. This is not just because of the dissolution of the Jewish priesthood but also from the effort of the early Christians to distance themselves from the dictates of the Mosaic Law. In the same way, the first councils of the Church (Nicea in A.D. 326, Constantinople in A.D. 381, Chalcedon in A.D 451; 2nd Constantinople in A. D 553), failed to give a unified treatise on tithing. However, due to the continued change in the nature of the priesthood, there were continued adjustments in the matters concerning the welfare of the priests. In the post-Nicene period we have some glimpses of teachings with regard to tithing. This section would be dedicated to the councils of Tours, Trent and Vatican II.

---

[28] Encyclopedia Britannica. 2006. Encyclopedia Britannica Premium Service. 4 June 2016, s.v. "tithe," http://www.britannica.com/eb/article-9072648).

6.3.1 The Council of Tours

Several councils were held in the city of Tours beginning from the fifth century. In the second Council of Tours, convoked by king Charibert and attended by nine bishops, tithing was advocated. At the end of the council, a letter was composed *ad plebem* of the province of Charibert, urging them vehemently to donate a tenth of their wealth and slaves to the church.[29] This means that we have a first positive appraisal of the need for the continued payment of tithe.

But before one would argue to the enduring nature of this legislation, it is well to note that it was also in this Council that it was decreed that a married bishop should treat his wife as a sister (canon XII). No priest or monk was to share his bed with someone else; and monks were not to have single or double cells, but were to have a common dormitory in which two or three were to take turns in staying awake and reading to the rest (canon XIV). If a monk married or had familiarity with a woman, he was to be excommunicated from the church until he returned penitent to the monastery enclosure and thereafter underwent a period of penance (canon XV). No woman was to be allowed to enter the monastery enclosure, and if anyone saw a woman enter and did not immediately expel her, he was to be excommunicated (canon XVI). Married priests, deacons and sub deacons should have their wives sleep together with the maidservants, while they themselves slept apart, and if anyone of them were found to be sleeping with his wife, he was to be excommunicated for a year and reduced to the lay state (canon XIX). These are some of the laws the nine bishops arrived at in 567.

These recommendations by the Council show the impact it has made in current practices in the Catholic Church. The decrees show that married priests were allowed to sleep with their wives before now; women were no longer allowed to enter into the monastery enclosure after this Council, etc. The decrees above also show that some of the

---

[29] Council of Tours (567) Synodal Letter.

practices are no longer tenable. For example, Catholic priests no longer marry. This is a transformation that was influenced by a change in the Catholic conception of the priesthood. The law is made for man.

6.3.2 The Council of Trent

The Council of Trent was the 19th ecumenical council of the Roman Church.[30] The main impulse for this council was to address the Reformation agenda and the issues that arose after the excommunication of Martin Luther. This Council witnessed two lengthy interruptions and much internal strife. Thus it was held in three parts from 1545 to 1563.[31] Nonetheless, it played important role in reforming the Roman Catholic Church from within. This Council accepted the Niceno-Constantinopolitan Creed as the basic faith of the Catholic Church, finalized the canon of the bible, accepted tradition and the Scriptures as the two sources of faith, declared that the Latin Vulgate was adequate for doctrinal proofs, fixed the number of the sacraments at seven. It also ruled against Luther's sola fide, etc.

With regard to our topic of discussion, the Council also made tremendous input. In the document of the Council of Trent, under the decree on reformation on the 4th of December, 1613, we read the following lines:

> Those are not to be borne who, by various artifices, endeavour to withhold the tithes accruing to the churches; nor those who rashly take possession of, and apply to their own use, the tithes which have to be paid by others; whereas the payment of tithes is due to God; and they who refuse to pay them, or hinder those who give them, usurp the property of another. Wherefore, the holy Synod

---

[30] It is here that one can begin to make a distinction between the teaching of the Catholic Church and the Protestant Movements. Before now, every discussion that has been made in this book concerns the whole of Christianity.

[31] Some of the problems encountered before and during the course of the Council have been studied by J. W. O'Malley, Trent, 2-6.

enjoins on all, of whatsoever rank and condition they be, to whom it belongs to pay tithes, that they henceforth pay in full the tithes, to which they are bound in law, to the cathedral church, or to whatsoever other churches, or persons, they are lawfully due. And they who either withhold them, or hinder them (from being paid), shall be excommunicated; nor be absolved from this crime, until after full restitution has been made. It further exhorts all and each, that, of their Christian charity, and the duty which they owe to their own pastors, they grudge not, out of the good things that are given them by God, to assist bountifully those bishops and parish priests who preside over the poorer churches; to the praise of God, and to maintain the dignity of their own pastors who watch for them.[32]

In the above citation we see that the tithe is to be paid in full and those who withhold the tithe are to be excommunicated. One has to understand the above edict from the general point of the council's appreciation of the importance of excommunication. Already in chapter three of the decree on reformation we read that the sword of excommunication is not to be used rashly. Hence pronouncing excommunication on those who fail to fulfil their obligation of tithing should be seen as one of the graver issues of the law according to the Council.

Writing in the year 1906, H. Lansdell concluded that the decrees of this Council "are binding on all Roman Catholics *till this day*."[33] Surely one is not to conclude that Lansdell meant that the decrees of this council are eternally binding. They were binding till the time of his writing and as a new law is promulgated, the binding effect ceases, just like most of the Mosaic Laws. And for those who would argue for the

---

[32] Council of Trent, December 4th 1613, Session XXV, Chapter XII.
[33] H. Lansdell, Sacred Tenth, 1:225. Emphasis added.

abiding status of the acts of this Council it is important to understand that the Council of Trent also commanded that the Eucharist should not be reserved within the enclosure of the convent. Again, the council directed that nuns should go to confession and receive communion once a month.[34] These are surely laws that have changed within the course of time. In this age, nobody is telling nuns how many times to receive communion or go to confession. There is now the pressing argument whether women should be admitted into the clerical state. The debate can go either way.

6.3.3 The Vatican II Council

When we turn to the documents of Vatican Council II, we witness the presence of general teachings on the dignity of the human person. Prominent among such teachings is the seminal document of Vatican Council II on the Declaration of Religious Freedom, *Dignitatis Humanae*. This declaration says much about the dignity of the human person and the rights of the worker to a just wage. It also connects the rights of the priest to the rights of the workers in general since the priest is a worker in God's vineyard.[35] This could be said to be the kernel of the Council's teaching on the care of the priest's temporal needs.

This kernel is then developed in the document on the Decree of the Ministry and Life of Priests, *Presbyterorum Ordinis*. Following the injunctions of Holy Scriptures and the teachings of earlier popes and Church Councils, section three of the document discusses the aids to the life of a priest. These aids include a deep and personal spiritual life (XVIII), constant study (XIX), ensuring equitable remuneration for priests (XX), and establishing social welfare for priests (XXI). About ensuring equitable remuneration for the priests, the document reasserts that the labourer deserves his wages (Lk 10:7) and that those who preach

---

[34] Cf. Council of Trent, Ch. X.
[35] J. I. Dolon, The Human Rights of Priests, 64.

the gospel should earn their living through the gospel (I Cor. 9:14).[36] The document also explains how this could be realized. The recommendations are important that they deserve some amount of space here:

> "the faithful themselves-that is, those in whose behalf the priest labors-are truly obliged to see to it that they can provide what help is necessary for the honorable and worthy life of the priests. The bishops, however, should admonish the faithful concerning this obligation of theirs. And they should see to if whether each individual for his own diocese or, more aptly, several together for their common territory-that norms are established according to which suitable support is rightly provided for those who do fulfill or have fulfilled a special office in the service of the People of God. The remuneration received by each one, in accord with his office and the conditions of time and place, should be fundamentally the same for all in the same circumstances and befitting his station. Moreover, those who have dedicated themselves to the service of the priesthood, by reason of the remuneration they receive, should not only be able to honorably provide for themselves but also themselves be provided with some means of helping the needy. For the ministry to the poor has always been held in great honor in the Church from its beginnings. Furthermore, this remuneration should be such that it will permit priests each year to take a suitable and sufficient vacation, something which indeed the bishops should see that their priests are able to have."[37]

It is evident that the above recommendations have summarized the bulk of our argument not only in this section but in the whole of this study. It

---

[36] Vatican II, Presbyterorum Ordinis, December 7, 1965, XX.
[37] Vatican II, Presbyterorum Ordinis, December 7, 1965, XX.

serves as a conciliar support of our thesis that each age and time should determine what it considers appropriate for the maintenance of her servants in the vineyard of the Lord. Reference to tithes and first fruits of the Old Law obscure the singularity and importance of the priesthood instituted by Christ. In the new dispensation, the care of the priests lies in the hands of the laity who should ensure that their servants have what should ensure their adequate living and also have some to carter for the poor that flock around them. Each diocesan bishop has an important role to play in this regard. The establishment of St. Vincent de Paul in several parishes, although helpful, may not be able to solve most of the needs of the poor that see the priest or pastor as the last place of refuge in the harsh realities that only grow grimmer in many countries of the world.

If the above discussion represents the conciliar decisions of the Church,[38] the encyclicals of individual popes clarify them. Under the social justice teaching of the Church inaugurated by Pope Leo XIII's *Rerum Novarum*, a new age dawned in the appraisal of means for the upkeep of the priests.

6.4 Adequate Support of the Clergy in Modern Papal Documents

Instead of the language of tithing and first fruits, one reads of the need for the adequate support of the clergy in modern teaching of the Catholic Church. There is a plethora of magisterial documents and pronouncements related to this issue. The whole concept can be encapsulated in the wider range of magisterial or ecclesial injunctions on social justice and the fact that the labourer deserves a just wage. As early as 1891, the issue of social justice has become a household concern in the church.

---

[38] It is evident that by Church we mean both the Church before the Reformation and the Church after. There is some level of continuity in the teachings about the care of the priests. The only difference seems to be in the epochal appreciation of the tenets of divine revelation.

On the 15th of May 1891, Pope Leo XIII issued *Rerum Novarum* which centered on the dignity and rights of workers. In defending the worker in the face of the disregard of human rights attendant on the industrialization in Europe and America, the Pontiff speaks against the continuous infringement of man's natural right, including his right to sound family and the right to adequate wages.[39] In this document, the just wage is defined as that which "must be enough to support the wage-earner in responsible and frugal comfort."[40] His incessant concern that the workers be paid a just wage could be used to imply that the priests who are workers in the Lord's vineyard should not be left out in this social justice system. On the heels of this document are several other magisterial writings like *Quadragesimo Anno* of Pius XI (1931), *Mater et Magistra* of Pope John XXIII (1961), *Populorum Progressio* of Paul VI (1967), *Sollicitudo Rei Socialis* of John Paul II (1987), among others.

Although the above documents focused on social justice on the general level, there were some other documents that made specific comments on the material support of the clergy. The initiative was taken in Pius XI's *Ad Catholici Sacerdotii*, issued on December 20th 1935. This document speaks eloquently about the holiness of the priesthood and the joy that comes from detachment from material things. It reminds the priest that "he is no mercenary working for a temporal recompense, nor yet an employee who, whilst attending conscientiously to duties of his office, at the same time is looking to his career and personal promotion."[41] Because of this, the priest is not to entangle himself in secular business. This is to enable him to be available and pleasing to God who has called him. But if this is the case, how is the priest to be sustained? The document also answers this question with recurs to the teaching of the NT. With implicit appeal to 1 Cor. 9:13, the pontiff

---

[39] Cf. C. O. Okwuru, Responsibilities and Significance, 282.
[40] Pope Leo XIII, Rerum Novarum, May 15, 1891. Quoted in C. O. Okwuru, Responsibilities and Significance, 282.
[41] Pope Pius XII, Ad Catholici Sacerdotii, December 20, 1935, 48.

points out that in the same way that "they that serve the altar may partake with the altar . . . so also the Lord ordained that they who preach the Gospel should live by the Gospel."[42] Although the nature of this living by the gospel is not defined by the pope, he makes it clear that nothing on earth could adequately pay the priest for the tremendous sacrifice his vocation calls him to offer. Therefore he should rejoice that his reward is great in heaven.

His initiative was followed by Pope Pius XII in his apostolic exhortation *Menti Nostrae*. Addressing the problem inherent in the maintenance of the clergy the pope asserts:

> But you will well understand that such a problem cannot be adequately resolved unless the faithful feel the obligation to help the clergy *according to their ability* and to take every step needed to achieve this end. Therefore instruct the faithful under your care on their obligation to help their priests in want...How can you expect fervent and energetic work from priests when they lack the necessities of life?[43]

In this statement, we see that the pope still maintains the apostolic injunction that the Christians should give according to their ability. It is an obligation which should be fulfilled without any compulsion. We also see that the era of tithes and first fruits now belong to the past. The exhortation also shows that the faithful help the priest in the fervent discharge of his responsibilities with their material support of the priest. Failure to do this on the part of the laity should be seen as failure in the mission.

In the second half of the 20th century, this teaching for the adequate care of the priest was emphasized. The encyclical of John XXIII, *Sacerdotii Nostri Primordia* of August 1st 1959 carried forth the concern

---

42 Pope Pius XII, Ad Catholici Sacerdotii, December 20, 1935, 48.
43 Pope Pius XII, Menti Nostrae, 63. Emphasis added.

for the welfare of the priest. He feels that the priest, as a matter of right, deserves equitable remuneration for his upkeep. For him, decent living does not amount to indigence on the part of the priest. Just like his predecessor did, the pope enjoined the faithful to be ardent in supporting their priests. In his words: "We share the feelings of our immediate predecessor in urging the faithful to respond quickly and generously to the appeal of their pastors; We also join him in praising these shepherds for their efforts to see to it that those who help them in the sacred ministry do not lack the necessities of life."[44] This document does not mention that salary should be paid to priests but stresses that the priest is entitled to the basic necessities of life.[45] We thus see a continuity of some keywords in these papal injunctions. What is to be underlined here are the three keywords: urging, generous and appeal. It is our opinion that these should be the guiding principles to any form of Christian giving for the good of those involved in propagating the message of the kingdom of God both in their active state and when they are retired.

6.5 The Code of Canon Law (1983) and Priestly Maintenance

We propose to discuss the code of the Canon Law of 1983 separately because it is the current code that regulates the practices of the Catholic Church. This code has something to say about previous universal or particular laws of the church in these words: When this Code takes force, the following are abrogated: 1. the Code of Canon Law promulgated in 1917; 2. other universal or particular laws contrary to the prescripts of this Code unless other provision is expressly made for particular laws; 3. any universal or particular penal laws whatsoever issued by the Apostolic See unless they are contained in this Code; 4. other universal disciplinary laws regarding matter which this Code

---

[44] Pope John XXIII, Ency. Letter, Sacerdotii Nostri Primordia, 14.
[45] Cf. James, The Human Rights of Priests, 56.

completely reorders. 5. Insofar as they repeat former law, the canons of this Code must be assessed also in accord with canonical tradition.[46]

With regard to our area of interest, the following canon and its prescriptions are important. Can. 222 §1 states that the Christian faithful are obliged to assist with the needs of the Church so that the Church has what is necessary for divine worship, for the works of the apostolate and of charity, and for the decent support of ministers. This is not the only Canon that makes explicit reference to the sustenance of priests. While reference could be made to canon 281 in its entirety, it is the first paragraph of that canon that concerns us here: "Since clerics dedicate themselves to the ecclesiastical ministry, they deserve the remuneration that befits their condition, taking into account both the nature of their office and the conditions of time and place. It is to be such that it provides for the necessities of their life and for the just remuneration of those whose services they need."[47] It is important to note that canon 281 is located in Book II that discusses the rights and responsibilities of the priest. This shows that what the priest receives as his remuneration is not charity to him. It is his right. But how is this right to be realized? In response to this question, the canon follows the teachings of Church Councils and popes. Paragraph one of canon 1274 establishes that it is the duty of every diocese to establish a special fund "in accordance with can. 281, for the support of the clergy who serve the diocese, unless they are otherwise provided for."[48]

In this respect, it might be important to clarify the provisions of the canon 281. This canon makes use of the word *rumenaratio* and not *stipendio*. Stipend can easily be seen as a fixed salary paid to a clergyman or public servant. The remuneration is a broader term. It includes the stipend and any other emolument that considers not only the

---

[46] J. P. Beal/J. A. Coriden/T. J. Green, Code of Canon Law (1983), Can. 6.

[47] J. P. Beal/J. A. Coriden/T. J. Green, The Code of Canon Law (1983), Can. 281, §1.

[48] J. P. Beal/J. A. Coriden/T. J. Green, The Code of Canon Law (1983), Can. 1274, §1.

volume or quantity of work done but also the person of the cleric who has given the whole of himself and his services to the work of the gospel. Actually, there is no way any church or organization can pay for the total given of a person to a mission. The priest is surely not like a civil servant who dedicates some part of his time to his occupation and the greater part to his personal needs. This explains why caring for his welfare is of utmost importance to the effectiveness of his mission.

6.6 Summary of Findings

This chapter focused on the practice of tithing or lack of it from the time of the Didache to the current Code of the Canon Law of 1983. We encountered the pronouncements of some ecumenical Councils and the teachings of a number of papal encyclicals. In some of these documents we find glimpses of the old relic of tithing and first fruits. This is especially the case with the Councils of Tours and Trent. As we found it in our enquiry, such teachings started taking effect from the 6th century, when Christianity has effectively established itself as the state religion in many European countries. But the majority of the documents of the early and later church fails to mandate the faithful as a matter of divine fiat to render a tithe of their belongings or earnings to God. There is surely the lack of the encouragement to pay the tithe. Most of the documents reviewed did not even mention tithe in any form. This is not surprising judging from the fact that the laws guiding the priesthood of the old order are radically different from the principles of the new priesthood. Again, the economic situations have changed and this demands a change in laws regarding the temporal care of the priests.

What we see is an encouragement to see to it that those who have devoted their entire lives to the service of the gospel are provided with the temporal necessities for the effective carrying out of their work. Each local church is mandated to formalize concrete ways of carrying out this objective in the spirit of equity. To the best of our knowledge, every diocese has got a plan for the maintenance of her priests. Whether these diocesan plans ensure an adequate maintenance of the priests is another question that should concern the financial committee of each diocese. Hence, there is a call for continuous renewal of current laws pertaining to priestly welfare.

CONCLUSION
TITHING AND HEAVENLY BLESSINGS

After much exegetical, theological and historical research, a study of this nature requires a good measure of hortatory balance. This is the stage where the insights gained from the book are *enfleshed* and served to those who have patiently followed its development. This section, therefore, deals with the idea of material blessing as following from a person's gifts to God. My colleagues from the Catholic Biblical Association of Nigeria (CABAN) have touched this issue in our 2014 edition of the Acts of CABAN.[1] Their discussions are still current.[2] We shall apply our findings in this book to the reality of a third world country, Nigeria.

For many years, mainstream Pentecostal or protestant churches in sing it as a mantra that lack of payment of the sacred tenth or the tithe blocks the flow of God's blessings to Christians. This teaching is hawked and retailed in all forms and shapes until now they have become literally accepted as dogma in these churches. It has also been adopted by many Catholic clergy and laity. Hence, many Christians pay their tithe as a way of drawing divine blessings and actually challenging God to perform miraculous things in their lives. This is how it plays out in the drama called Nigeria. It is also the case in many other underdeveloped countries. In climes where no attention is paid to equity and where people have to be involved in series of settlements or bribes in order to get what should rightfully be theirs, it is easy to see how the

---

[1] B. Ukwuegbu, et al (eds.), "Material Wealth and Divine Blessings in the Bible" Acts of the Catholic Biblical Association of Nigeria (CABAN), Vol.5 (2014). Two contributors to this volume focused exclusively on the tithe. Cf. V. Onwukeme, "Scriptural Basis for the Tithe and Tax," 1-13; C. U. Manus, "Tithing: Wealth Creation for some Pastors vis a vis the Pauperization of the Faithful," 139-157.

[2] Another colleague has offered a recent summarized and reflective study of some of the issues in this book. See B. Ugwu, Tithe and Tithing in our Churches Today. Enugu, 2016.

145

affairs in the temporal realm are transferred to the divine realm. We have explained elsewhere how this settlement works:

> "It normally involves a chain of connections. Most times, this connection is achieved through the agency of bribery or kickbacks. It is not uncommon that students have their exams taken for them by professors or the results fixed for them even when they did not partake in the exams. Securing reasonable employment is often a result of paying several rounds of bribes to both relevant and irrelevant bodies. As a contractor, getting a meaningful contract always involves the same modus of bribery and corruption... In the political realm, it goes beyond description. One must have a god-father or more appropriately a demon-father to secure any position of importance."[3]

This is the reality of life many have plunged themselves into. Many scholars would term this systemic evil but it would be good to realize that nothing enters into the system that did not begin from the individual. However one looks at this phenomenon, it has led to a situation whereby God is drawn into the moral evil of bribery and corruption in the name of tithe. Tithing has become a way of bribing God into action. It is not difficult to see how God becomes corrupt in a corrupt environment. After all it was the angelic doctor who formulated this *non dubitandum* statement that the received is in the receiver according to the mode of the receiver.[4] This means that humans always try to make reality to fit their worldview. This explains the insistence on the payment of tithe as a way of drawing down God's blessings as if material gifts win God over.

This cannot be true based on the scriptural passages we have examined. We have seen that the offertory of Cain and Abel (Gen 4:3-5)

---

[3] R. Onyenali, Hebrew Women, 40f.
[4] Cf. Thomas Aquinas, Summa Theologica, 1a, q. 75, a. 5; 3a, q. 5.

has nothing to do with tithing. We have seen that Abram's payment of tithe to Melchizedek occurred after he had received the blessing from the priest-king of Salem (Gen 14:18-20). Again, what Abram offered is a tithe of the booty he got and not a tithe of his personal belonging or earning. The promise made to Abraham was based on faith and not on his offering of tithe (Gen 12:1-3; Rom 4:13-16). Also, the vow of Jacob to offer a tithe (Gen 28:20) was based on the condition that God already blesses him and makes him return safely to his father land. In the two episodes of Abram and Jacob, the blessing preceded the tithe. And in the case of Jacob we are not told whether or not he paid the tithe. When we turn to the Mosaic injunctions, we find no explicit connection between the offering of tithe and divine blessings to the offerer. Although it could be taken that such fulfilment of divine mandates should be followed by divine blessing. However, this connection between the offering of tithe and divine blessing is not made clearly in the Jewish Law. In Tobit (1:7) we read that Tobit paid his tithe. Yet it did not prevent him from going blind and experiencing other ills of human existence. It is only in the words of the prophet Malachi (3:10) that such explicit connection is made between tithe and blessing. Our studies have shown that the referent to the injunction was the High Priest in whose care was the store house of the Temple meant to contain the tithes of the Levites. This store house has been emptied leading to the exit of the Levites. In a situation whereby the servants of God have abandoned their tasks due to lack of the necessary aids to their service, one understands how divine blessings would be deferred until the wrongs are made right. This is surely in agreement with fundamental spirituality. Therefore, the High Priest Eliashib, under whose watch the store room for Levitical tithes has been emptied, was asked to return the tithes so that normal worship can be carried out in the Temple. Using this passage by the priests or pastors to preach the payment of tithe to the priest or pastor is nothing but double robbery.

Insistence on the payment of tithe and the divine goodies attendant on it while neglecting the weightier issues of the law like justice, hard work and love can only produce negative results. This is where we can venture to propose some teachings that could draw down divine blessings on the people more than the payment of tithe. We begin with the education sector. The anomalies in the Nigerian education sector are too many to be discussed here.[5] It is no secret that the building or destruction of a society has a lot to do with the education or lack of it present in this society. Neglect to build up the intellectual and moral aptitudes of the younger generation is tantamount to conscious effort to uproot the society. We dare to say that sound education which involves the rational, affective and actional aspects of the human person is the proper way to achieving the godly bliss which many years of tithing has not achieved and would never achieve. As early as 1898 a Lagos Governor observed that most of the clerks supplied by the secondary schools in Lagos were illiterate and ignorant and that a radical change was imperative.[6] If this could be said about education in Nigeria during the colonial era, one does not need to be wise in any sense to conclude that education has been eroded in the various cadres of learning in the country as at the time of writing.[7] It does not mean that the country does not have the ability. There is a clear absence of goodwill to do what is right. Therefore bring all the educational capabilities of the nation into the classroom and see whether God will not destroy the illiteracy and militancy that have bedeviled your land. This should involve the

---

[5] See G. A. Fabure, "Anomalies in Nigeria's Educational System," as quoted in J. S. Coleman, Nigeria, 116. See also H. Peets, "Kolonialpolitik," In: H. N. Weiler (ed.) Erziehung, 96f; Sir A. Burns, Nigeria, 270; R. Onyenali, Cognitive Approach, 89-92.

[6] Cf. E. A. Ayandele, Missionary Impact, 294.

[7] For studies on the low quality of education in modern day Nigeria see D. Omotayo, et al, Management, 7; S. O. Alaba, "Improving the Standard and Quality of Primary Education in Nigeria: A Case Study of Oyo and Osun States," in: International Journal for Cross-Disciplinary Subjects in Education (IJCDSE), Volume 1, Issue 3, September 2010.

abrogation of certificates given to schools that obviously lack the ability and will to be outstanding in this area. On the part of the teachers there should be the readiness to insist on acceptable standard before a student could be allowed to acquire any form of certificate from the school concerned. If our loud speakers could trumpet this at every church service, we would gain more than what several years of tithing has failed to achieve.

The problem of low quality education affects everything in the life of a nation. There is surely a clear connection between low intellectual development and a low level of moral appreciation of reality.[8] Most of our graduates and those who allowed them to graduate still have their minds filled with superstitious and magical ideas. One needs only watch our news and home videos to see how almost everything that occurred in the developed countries in the middle ages is occupying centre stage among us. Ours is a situation whereby people who are supposed to be drop outs end up being the leaders, prophets, and seers of the society. This has grave consequences.

Let us begin with the area of leadership or politics. We have argued elsewhere that "the processes of decision-making and the use of information involved in the democratic process may be too complex to be appreciated in an illiterate milieu."[9] In this state of affairs, the voters lack the required competence to distinguish the candidates and their manifestoes. Hence, the choice of the electorate is based on the candidate suggested to them by their village chiefs[10] or by those who are ready to afford them some cups of rice. This could be one of the major problems affecting the democratic process in many third world countries. The political class then sees the masses as their subjects

---

[8] See the studies of F. Oser/P. Gmünder, Entwicklung des Menschen, 128-40; F. Oser/P. Gmünder, Der Mensch, 15.

[9] R. Onyenali, Cognitive Approach, 95.

[10] An interview carried out by J. P. Mackintosh in 1961 showed this tendency. His findings are quoted in P. E. Ollawa, Demokratie, 210.

instead of citizens. G. Almond and S. Verba see a subject as a "passive beneficiary or victim of routine governmental actions...What the government does affects him, but why or how the government decides to do what it does is outside his sphere of competence" while the citizen, on the other hand, is "expected to take an active part in governmental affairs, to be aware of how decisions are made, and to make his views known."[11] Almond and Verba concluded that "if decision makers believe that the ordinary man could participate...they are likely to behave quite differently than if such a belief did not exist. Even if individuals do not act according to this belief, decision makers may act on the assumption that they can, and in this way be more responsive to the citizenry than they would be if the myth of participation did not exist."[12] This submission is very correct in the Nigerian situation. In his *Path to Nigerian Freedom*, one of the foremost founders of Nigeria, makes the following remarks: "as for the remaining masses, they are ignorant and will not be bothered by politics. Their sole preoccupation is to search for food, clothing and shelter of a wretched type. To them, it does not matter who rules the country, so long as in the process they are allowed to live their lives in peace and curd comfort. If they bestir themselves at all, as they do occasionally, it is because they have been unduly oppressed by a tribal chieftain, or outraged by the blunders of an administrative officer."[13] Although this statement was made many years ago, the reality still remains the same.

If we consider the religious atmosphere, the abysmal level of education stinks to the highest heavens. Our graduates are experts in preaching the bible which they neither studied nor understood. We have a rich harvest of prophets who declare divine blessings on people just for typing "amen" to some hopeless Facebook posts that lack content.

---

[11] Quoted in P. E. Ollawa, Demokratie, 211.
[12] Quoted in P. E. Ollawa, Demokratie, 212.
[13] O. Awolowo, Path to Nigerian Freedom, 31.

The self-acclaimed men and women of God market their well-fabricated myths and term them divine mandates. And because there are no adequate rational checks and balances, they turn the Scriptures on its head and dish out the unhealthy pills of ignorance and unfounded prophecies on the gullible public. These pills are swallowed as medicine. In the course of time they gradually eat up the inner tissues of faith and godly living. The result is that the people perish because of lack of understanding. But if the younger generation is rationally equipped, they would be able to subject any sort of teaching to rigorous investigation before falling prey to demonic agents in clerical garb.[14] Obviously, one cannot serve two masters at the same time. You cannot be preaching the Law of Moses and pretend to be living under the grace of Christ.

This does not mean that we do not have places in our Scriptures that narrate the relationship between giving and blessing. In Lk 6:38, these words are reported of Jesus: "give and you shall be given." As we have also explained elsewhere, it is very important for the reader or the interpreter of this passage to point out that because of Luke's incessant option for the poor, he is admonishing his community to be generous to the poor. Luke's intention is to let us know that the more we give to the poor the more God blesses us with full measures pressed and running down our laps.[15] This option for the poor sums up the ministry and life of Jesus and those of his immediate followers.

It is now time for us to refer back to the stories at the introduction of this book. God does not rely on your faithful recitation of a fixed

---

[14] According to M. E. Narramore, "the devil doesn't mind tithing. He welcomes anything that will take our attention away from the truth in Christ." See his Tithing: Low Realm, Obsolete and Defunct, 1. For Narramore, tithing is like the legendary Trojan horse that apparently was a gift of the gods but possessed only the agents of destruction. In fact, he calls tithing a low-realm spirituality while calling on the church to make a paradigm shift in the mode of giving.

[15] Cf. R. Onyenali, Hebrew Women, 42.

formula of prayer and adoration to answer your prayers. This is shown in the lives of Rabbis Israel Baal Shem-Tov, Magid of Mazeritch, Moshe-Leib of Sassove, and Israel of Rizhin. The increasing failure to recite the ancient creed and to follow the old ritual did not hamper the miracle. In the same way, knowledge of the reason why the Zen Buddhist master, who was in charge of the Mayu Kagi monastery, tied his cat before meditation is necessary to knowing whether the cat is necessary at all for effective meditation. Failure to know this would amount to pouring new wine into old wineskin. The loss would be colossal. This is what the disciples of *titheology* often forget.

BIBLIOGRAPHY

1. PRIMARY SOURCES

1.1. BIBLES AND SYNOPSES

Biblia Hebraica Stuttgartensia. Deutsche Bibelgesellschaft, (hrsg.), ^{5}1997.
Aland, B./K. Aland, K. et al. (hrsg.), Novum Testamentum Graece. Stuttgart ^{27}1994.
Robinson, J. M./Hoffmann, P./Kloppenborg, S. (eds.), The Critical Edition of Q. Synopsis including the Gospel of Matthew and Luke, Mark and Thomas, with English, German, and French Translations of Q and Thomas. Peeters, 2000.
Aland, B./Aland, K. et at, (eds.), The UBS Greek New Testament: A Reader's Edition.. Stuttgart: Deutsche Bibelgesellschaft, 2007.

1.2 ANCIENT GREEK AND ROMAN SOURCES

Aquinas, Thomas, Summa Theologica. First Complete American Edition in Three Volumes (trans. by Fathers of the English Dominican Province). New York, 1947.
Aristotle: Aristotle, LCL, (23 vols.), Massachusetts/London, 1926-1975.
Dio Chrysostom, Dio Chrysostom, with an English Translation, I.II by J.W. Cohoon, III by J.W. Cohoon/H.L. Crosby, IV.V by H.L. Crosby, LCL, London/Massachusetts, 1961-1964.
Flavius Josephus: The Jewish War, LCL, trans. by H.St.J.Thackeray, Massachusetts/London, 1976.
Flavius Josephus: With an English Trans., LCL, IV-IX Jewish

Antiquities, IV.V by R. Marcus/A. Wilkgren, IX by L.H. Feldman, Massachusetts/London, 1961-1969.

Herodotus, with an English translation by Godley, A. D. Cambridge, 1920.

Lucian Works with an English Translation by Harmon, A. M. Cambridge/London,1921.

Philo of Alexandria: The Works of Philo, complete and unabridged. Trans. C.D. Yonge, Massachusetts, 1993.

Procopius, History of the Wars, Books V. and VI, with English translation by H. B. Dewing. Release Date: January 6, 2007 [EBook #20298].

Sophocles, Trachinia with English Notes by P. A. Paley, London, 1880.

1.3 DICTIONARIES AND CONCORDANCE

Arndt, W., et al., A Greek-English lexicon of the New Testament and Other Early Christian Literature. 2000.

Betz, H. D. (hrsg.), Religion in Geschichte und Gegenwart (RGG). Handwörterbuch für Theologie und Religionswissenschaft, (8 Bd.). Tübingen, 1998-2005.

Brown, F/ Driver, S. R/Briggs, C. A., A Hebrew and English Lexicon of the Old Testament with an appendix containing the biblical Aramaic (BDB). Oxford: Clarendon, 1907.

Bottlerweck, G. J/Ringgren, H/Fabry H-J (eds), Theological Dictionary of the Old Testament (Vol. 11). Translated by Green D. E. Grand Rapids, 2001.

Davis, J. D. (ed.), Westminster Dictionary of the Bible. Philadelphia, 1964.

Freedman, D. N. (ed), The Anchor Bible Dictionary, Vol. 6. New York, 1922.

Guthrie, H. H., The Interpreters Dictionary of the Bible (vol.4).
        New York-Nashville, 1962.
Hastings, J. (ed), Encyclopedia of Religion and Ethics. Edinburgh, 1980.
Kittel, G./Friedrich, G., Theologisches Wörterbuch zum Neuen
        Bd.). Tübingen, 1998-2005.
McKenzie, J. L., Dictionary of the Bible. London, 1965.
McClintock, J./Strong, J. (eds.) The Cyclopedia of Biblical, Theological,
        and Ecclesiastical Literature Vol. X. New York, 1880.
Myers, A. C. The Eerdmans Bible Dictionary. Grand Rapids, 1987.
Singer, I. (ed.), The Jewish Encyclopedia, Vol. 12. Jerusalem, 1901.
Smith, W. R. (ed.), Encyclopedia Britannica (in many volumes).
Thomas, R. L (ed.), New American Standard Hebrew-Aramaic and
        New American Standard Hebrew-Aramaic and Greek
        Dictionaries. Updated Edition by Thomas R. L., Anaheim, CA,
        1998.
Unger, M. F (ed.), The New Unger's Bible Dictionary. Chicago, 1988.

2. SECONDARY SOURCES

2.1 COMMENTARIES

Barclay, W., The Letter to the Hebrews. Edinburgh, 1976.
Beal, J. P/Coriden, J. A/Green, T. J. (eds.), New Commentary of the
        Code of Canon Law. New York, 2000.
Bultmann, R., The Gospel of John. Philadelphia, 1971.
Childs, B. S., The Book of Exodus: A Critical, Theological
        Commentary, Old Testament Library. Philadelphia, 1974.
Clendenen, R. E., Haggai-Malachi. The New American Commentary:
        An Exegetical and Theological Exposition of Holy Scripture
        (vol. 21A). Nashville, 2004.
Cockerill, G. L., The Epistle to the Hebrews. (NICNT), Grand Rapids/

Cambridge, 2012.

Craigie, P. C., Twelve Prophets: Micah, Nahum, Habbakuk, Zephaniah, Zechariah, and Malachi. Louisville, 1985.

Cranfield, C. E. B., The Gospel According to Saint Mark. Cambridge, 1963.

Davies, W. D/Allison, D. C. Jr., A Critical and Exegetical Commentary on the Gospel According to Saint Matthew, ICC (3 vols.). Edinburgh, 1988-1997.

Delitzsch, F., A New Commentary on Genesis (2 vols.), translated by Sophia Taylor, reprint of 1888 ed. Minneapolis, 1978.

Driver, S. R., The Book of Genesis. London, 1904.

Gunkel, H., Genesis. Macon, GA, 1997.

Hagner, D. A., Matthew, (2 vols.), WBC. Dallas, 1993/1995.

Hamilton, V. P., The Book of Genesis (2 vols.), NICOT. Grand Rapids, 1990/1995.

Keil, C. F., and Franz Delitzsch. *The Pentateuch* (3 vols.). Translated by James Martin. Biblical Commentary on the Old Testament. N.p.; reprint ed., Grand Rapids, 1884.

Kent, H. A., The Epistle to the Hebrews. Grand Rapids, 1972.

Lane, W. L., Hebrews 1-8 (WBC 47a). Columbia, 1991.

Lundblom, J. R., Deuteronomy: A Commentary. Grand Rapids. 2013.

Luz, U., Das Evangelium nach Matthäus, EKK 1/1-4. Neukirchen-Vluyn. 1985/1990/1997/2002.

Matthews, K. A., Genesis 1:1-11:26, NAC. Nashville, 1996.

Milgrom, J., Leviticus 17—*22*. (AncB). New York, 2000.

Milgrom, J., Leviticus 23-27: A New Translation with Introduction and Commentary (The Anchor Bible). New York, 2001.

Milavec, A., The Didache: Text, Translation, Analysis and Commentary. Minnesota, 2003.

Nolan, B. H. (ed.), The Interpreter's Bible (vol. 1). Nashville, 1954.

Noordtzij, A. Leviticus. Translated by Raymond Togtman (BSCS).

Grand Rapids, 1982.

Petersen, D. L., Zechariah 9-14 & Malachi. Old Testament Library. Louisville, 1995.

Rad, G. von, Genesis. A Commentary (rev. ed.). Philadelphia, 1972.

Rooker, M. F., Leviticus. (NAC). Nashville, 2000.

Simpson, C. A., Genesis. Interpreter's Bible, G. Buttrick (ed.). New York, 1962.

Skinner, J., A Critical and Exegetical Commentary on Genesis, (ICC). Edinburgh, 1910.

Speiser, E. A., Genesis, (2nd ed.). AB (Garden City, NY, 1978.

Stuart, D., The Minor Prophets: An Exegetical and Expository Commentary (vol. 13). Grand Rapids, MI, 1998.

Sweeney, M. A., The Twelve Prophets: Micah Nahum, Zephaniah, Haggai, Zechariah, Malachi (vol. 2), Berit Olam series. Collegeville, MN, 2001.

Taylor, R. A/Clendenen, E. R., Haggai, Malachi: An Exegetical and Theological Exposition of Holy Scripture (NAC). Nashville, 2004.

Verhoef, P. A., The Books of Haggai and Malachi (NICOT). Grand Rapids, 1987.

Wenham, G. J., Genesis 1-15 (WBC 1). Columbia, 1987.

Wenham, G. J., The Book of Leviticus (NICOT). Grand Rapids, 1979.

Westermann, C., Genesis (3 vols.), Continental Commentaries. Minneapolis: Augsburg, 1984.

2. 2 BOOKS AND MONOGRAPHS

Aelred C., A History of Old Testament Priesthood. Rome, 1969.

Albertz, R., A History of Israelite Religion in the Old Testament Period, Volume II: From the Exile to the Maccabees. Göttingen, 1992.

Allan P. Ross, Holiness to the Lord: A Guide to the Exposition of the

Book of Leviticus. Grand Rapids, 2002.

Anderson, G. A., Sacrifice and Sacrificial Offering, *ABD*, D. N. Freedman (ed.). New York, 1997.

----------, Sacrifices and Offerings in Ancient Israel: Studies in their Social and Political Importance (Harvard Semitic Monographs 41). Atlanta, 1987.

Antonius, H. J. Gunneweg, Leviten und Priester, Göttingen, 1965.

Aptowitzer, V., Kain und Abel in der agada: den Apokryphen, der hellenistischen, christlichen und muhammedanischen Literatur. Wien/Leipzig, 1922.

Aquinas, Thomas, Summa

Awolowo, O., Path to Nigerian Freedom. 1974.

Ayandele, E. A., The Missionary Impact on Modern Nigeria 1842-1914: A Political and Social Analysis. London, 1966.

Biale, D., Blood and Belief: The Circulation of a Symbol Between Jews and Christians. Berkeley, 2007.

Blackman, E. C., Marcion and his Influence. London, 1948.

Borg, M., Meeting Jesus Again for the First Time. San Francisco, 1994.

Bratcher, D. R., Torah as Holiness: Old Testament Law as Response to Divine Grace. Ohio, 1994.

Brice, L. L., Greek Warfare: From the Battle of Marathon to the Conquests of Alexander the Great. California, 2012.

Bright, J. Early Israel in Recent History Writing. London, 1956.

Bryon, J. Cain and Abel in Text and Tradition: Jewish and Christian Interpretations of the First Sibling Rivalry. Leiden, 2011.

Bush, G., *Notes, Critical and Practical, on the Book of Leviticus.* New York, 1852/Minneapolis, 1976.

Candlish, R. S., An Exposition of Genesis. Wilmington, DE, 1972.

Chafer, L.S., Major Bible Themes. Chicago, 1944.

Charlesworth. J. H. (ed.), The Old Testament Pseudepigrapha. New York, 1985.

Coelho, P., Like the Flowing River: Thoughts and Reflections. London, 2007.

Coleman, J. S., Nigeria: Background to Nationalism. Berkeley/Los Angeles, 1960.

Comber, T., The Historic Vindication of the Divine Right of Tithes. 1682.

Contenau, G., Everyday Life in Babylon and Assyria. New York, 1954.

Cross, F. M/Freedman, D. N., Studies in Ancient Yahwist Poetry. Grand Rapids, 1997.

Crossan, J. D., The Historical Jesus: The Life of a Mediterranean Peasant. San Francisco, 1993.

Dahlberg, B. T., Studies in the Book of Malachi. Columbia University PhD diss. 1963.

De Vaux, R., *An Ancient Israel*, Its Life and Institutions, London, 1961.

De Wette, W. M. L., Beiträge zur Einleitung in das Alte Testament (2 vols.). Halle, 1806, 1807.

Dolon, J. I., The Human Rights of Priests to Equitable Sustenance and Mobility : An Examination of Canon Law from the Codex Iuris Canonici to the Proposed Revision of the Code of Canon Law. Diss, 1983.

Donner, H., Geschichte des Volkes Israel und Seiner Nachbarn in Grundzügen: Teil 1: Von den Anfängen bis zur Staatenbildungszeit. Götting, 2007.

Draper, J. A./Jefford, C. N., The Didache: A Missing Piece of the Puzzle in Early Christianity. Atlanta, 2015.

Duhm, B., Die Theologie der Propheten als Grundlage für die innere Entwicklungsgeschichte der israelitischen Religion. 1875/2011.

Dumbrell, W. J., Covenant and Creation: A Theology of Old Testament Covenants. Nashville, 1984.

Dunn, J. D. G., Jesus, Paul and the Law: Studies in Mark and Galatians.

Westminster, 1990.

Engnell, I., Studies in Divine Kingship in the Ancient Near East Oxford, 1967.

Erman, A., Life in Ancient Egypt. London/New York, 1894.

Fant, C. E/Reddish, M. G., Lost Treasures of the Bible: Understanding the Bible Through Archaeological Artifacts in World Museums. Grand Rapids, 2008.

Fee, G. D/Stuart, D., How to Read the Bible for All its Worth, Grand Rapids, 1981.

Finegan, J., Light from the Ancient Past (vol. 1): The Archeological Background of the Hebrew-Christian Religion. Princeton, 1946.

Finkelstein, L., The Pharisees: The Sociological Background of Their Faith (3rd ed.). Philadelphia, 1962.

Gane R. E/Cohen, A. T. (ed), Current Issues in Priestly and Related Literature: The Legacy of Jacob Milgrom and Beyond (SBL 82), 2015.

Gilders, W. K., Blood Ritual in the Hebrew Bible: Meaning and Power. Baltimore/London, 2004.

Grabbe, L. L., Judaic Religion in the Second Temple Period: Belief and Practice from the Exile to Yavneh. London, 2000.

Gray, G. B., Sacrifice in the Old Testament: Its Theory and Practice New York, 1971.

Grypeou, E/Spurling, H., The Book of Genesis in Late Antiquity: Encounters between Jewish and Christian Exegesis. Leiden, 2013.

Hahn, S. W., Kingship by Covenant: A Canonical Approach to the Fulfilment of God's Saving Promises. New Haven/London, 2009.

Hallo, W. W., Context of Scripture (3 vols.). Leiden, 2002.

Hammond, P. C., The Nabataeans—Their History, Culture and Archaeology, SMA 37 (Gothenburg, 1973).

Haran, M., Temples and Temple-service in Ancient Israel: An Inquiry into Biblical Cult Phenomena and the Historical Setting of the Priestly School. Oxford, 1978.

Hardin, J. K., Galatians and the Imperial Cult (WUNT 2. R 237). Tübingen, 2008.

Haenchen, E., Der Weg Jesu: Eine Erklärung des Markus-Evangeliums und der kanonischen Parallelen. 2. Durchgesehene u. verbesserte Auflage. Berlin, 1968.

Herrman, S., Israels Aufenthalt in Ägypten. Stuttgart, 1970.

Herrman, S., A History of Israel in Old Testament Times. Philadephia, 1981.

Hietanen, M., Paul's Argumentation in Galatians: A Pragma-Dialectical Analysis (LNTS 344). New York, 2007.

Hill, A. E., "Dating the Book of Malachi: A Linguistic Reexamination": In Meyers/O'Connor (eds.) The Word of the Lord Shall Go Forth: Essays in Honour of D. N. Freedman in Celebration of His Sixtieth Birthday. Winona Lake, 1983, 77-89.

Horton, F. L., The Melchizedek Traditions: A Critical Examination of the Sources to the Fifth Century A.D. And in the Epistle to the Hebrews. Cambridge, 1976.

House, P. R., Old Testament Theology. Downers Grove, 1998.

James, The Human Rights of Priests.

Jefford, C. N., The Teaching of the Twelve Apsotles: Didache. Santa Rosa, 2013.

Jenson, P. P., Graded Holiness: A Key to the Priestly Conception of the World (JSOT.S, 106). Sheffield, 1992.

Joosten, J., People and Land in the Holiness Code: An Exegetical Study of Ideational Framework of the Law in Leviticus 17-26, Leiden, 1966.

Kelly, R. E., Should the Church Teach Tithing?: A Theologian's Conclusions about a Taboo Doctrine. Lincoln, 2007.

Kendall, R. T., Tithing: A Call to Serious, Biblical Giving. Grand
	Rapids, 1982.

Kim, L., Polemic in the book of Hebrews: Anti-Judaism, Anti-Semitism,
	Supersessionism? (PTMS 64). Pickwick, 2006.

Knox, J., Marcion and the New Testament. Chicago, 1942.

Konradt, M., Israel, Kirche und die Völker im Matthäusevangelium
	(WUNT 215). Tübingen, 2007.

Lansdell, H., Sacred Tenth: Or Studies in Tithe Giving Among Ancient
	and Modern. Grand Rapids, 1955.

Langdon, S., Die Neubabylonischen Königsinschriften, Vorderasiatische
	Bibliothek 4. Leipzig, 1912.

Lemche, N. P., Die Vorgeschichte Israels (Biblische Enzyklopädie, I).
	Stuttgart, 1996.

Letts, J., A Succinct History of Tithe in London : Shewing the Progress
	of that Portion of the Ecclesiastical Revenues, from a very Early
	Period. Cornhill, 1824.

Lichtheim, M., Ancient Egyptian Literature, III: The Late Period.
	Berkeley, 1980.

Longman, T., III/Dillard, R. B., *An Introduction to the Old Testament.*
	(2nd ed.). Grand Rapids, 2006.

Luckenbill, D. D., The Annals of Sennachrib, The University of Chicago
	Oriental Institute Publications (vol.2). Chicago, 1924.

Maspero, The Struggle of the Nations: Egypt, Syria and Assyria.
	London, 1896.

Martinez, P. G., The Dead Sea Scrolls and Pauline Literature, Ed Jean-
	Sebastien Rey (STDJ 102). Leiden, 2014.

McConville, J. G., Law and Theology in Deuteronomy (JSOT.S 33).
	Sheffield, 1984.

McNamara, Palestinian Judaism and the New Testament. Wilmington,
	1983.

Milavec, A., The Didache: Faith, Hope, & Life of the Earliest Christian

Communities. 50-70 CE. New York, 2003.

Milgrom, J., Sacrifices and Offerings, OT, IBD Supplementary Volume, K. Crim (Ed). Nashville, 1976.

Narramore, M. E., Tithing: Low Realm, Obsolete and Defunct. Graham, 2004.

Neusner, J., The Rabbinic Traditions about the Pharisees before 70 (3 vols). Leiden, 1971.

Nicholson, E. W., God and his People: Covenant and Theology in the Old Testament. Oxford, 1986.

North, W., Christian Writing Decoded: The Didache. LLC, 2012.

Okwuru, C. O., The Responsibilities and Significance of the Congregatio pro Clericis in the Life and Ministry of the Diocesan Clergy. 2012.

Ollawa, P. E., Demokratie und nationale Integration in Nigeria. Frankfurt, 1973.

O'Malley, J. W., Trent: What Happened at the Council. Harvard, 2013.

Omotayo, D/Ihebereme, M/Maduewesi, B. U., Management of Universal Basic Education (UBE). High Beam Research, 2008.

Onwuka, P. C., The Law, Redemption and Freedom in Christ: An Exegetical-Theological Study of Galatians 3,10-14 and Romans 7,1-6 (TGST 156). Roma, 2007.

Onyenali, R., Appraising the Nigerian Problem Through Education and Religious Dialogue: A Cognitive Approach. Frankfurt, 2013.

----------, Matthew's Gospel as Enculturated Narrative. Lagos, 2015.

----------, The Trilogy of Parables in Mt 21:28-22:14: From a Matthean Perspective. Frankfurt, 2013.

Oser, F/Gmünder, P., Der Mensch-Stufen seiner religiösen Entwicklung. Ein strukturgenetischer Einsatz (2. Überarb. Aufl). Gütersloh, 1988.

Oswald L., Ugarit und die Bibel. Kanaanäische Götter und Religion im Alten Testament. Darmstadt, 1990.

Brooke, G. J., Ugarit and the Bible. Proceedings of the International Symposium on Ugarit and the Bible, Manchester, September 1992 (UBL 11). Münster, 1994.

Overman, J. A., Matthew's Gospel and Formative Judaism: The Social World of the Matthean Community. Minneapolis, 1955.

Pope, M., El in the Ugaritic Texts. Leiden, 1955.

Powers, T. J., An Historical Study of the Tithe in the Christian Church to 1648. Phd Diss. Southern Baptist Theological Seminary, 1948.

Pritchett, W. K., The Greek State at War I. Berkeley, 1971.

Quesnell, Q., The Mind of Mark: Interpretation and Method through the Exegesis of Mark 6,52 (AnBib 38). Rome, 1969.

Rapa, R. K., The Meaning of "Works of the Law in" in Galatians and Romans (StudBL 31). New York, 2001.

Riedl, G., Model Assisi: Christliches Gebet und interreligiöser Dialog in heilsgeschichtlichem Kontext. Berlin/New York, 1998.

Rivkin, E., A Hidden Revolution. Nashville, 1978.

Ross, A. P., Creation & Blessing: A Guide to the Study and Exposition of Genesis. Grand Rapids, 1988.

Rouse, W. H. D., Greek Votive Offerings: An Essay in the History of Greek Religion. Cambridge, 1902.

Rowley, H. H., Worship in Ancient Israel. Philadelphia, 1967.

Sanders, E. P., Jewish Law from Jesus to the Mishnah. London, 1990.

Sandmel, S., Anti-Semitism in the New Testament? Philadelphia, 1978.

Scarlata, M. W., Outside of Eden: Cain in the Ancient Versions of Genesis 4.1-16. London/New York, 2012.

Schaper, J., Priester und Leviten im achämenidischen Juda: Studien zur Kult- und Socialgeschichte Israels in persischer Zeit (FAT 31). Tübingen, 2000.

Schiffman, L. H., The Courtyards of the House of the Lord: Studies on Temple Scroll. Leiden, 2008.

Schürer, E/Vermes, G/Millar, F/Goodman, M., The History of the

Jewish People in the Age of Jesus Christ III I. Edinburgh, 1986.
Selden, J., History of Tithes. 1618.
Simon, M., Jewish Sects at the Time of Jesus, trans. James H. Farley. Philadelphia, 1967.
Skehan, P. W., The Wisdom of Ben Sira. New York, 1987.
Smith, R., Lectures on the Religion of the Semites 2nd and 3rd Series (JSOT.S 183). Sheffield, 1894.
Steinmetz, D., From Father to Son: Kingship, Conflict and Continuity in Genesis. Westminster, 1991.
Suton, J., Another More Excellent Way: This they shall Give. USA, 2009.
Thompson, J. A., The Ancient Near Eastern Treaties and the Old Testament. London, 1964.
Ugwu, B., Tithe and Tithing in our Churches Today. Enugu, 2016.
Tiemeyer, L-S., Priestly Rites and Prophetic Rage: Post-exilic Prophetic Critique of the Priesthood (FZAT 2. Reihe, 19). Tübingen, 2006.
Van der Merwe, J-A. I., An Exegetical and Theological Study of Malachi 3:8-12 And its Implications for Christians, with Particular Reference to Tithing (Master's Thesis). Seattle, 2010.
Van Seters, J., Abraham in History and Tradition. New Haven, 1975.
Volkes, F. E., The Riddle of the Didache: Fact or Fiction, Heresy or Catholicism? London, 1938.
Von Hanack, A., Marcion: Das Evangelium vom fremden Gott (2nd ed). Leipzig, 1924.
Von Orelli, C., The Twelve Minor Prophets. Minneapolis, 1977.
Von Rad, G., Old Testament Theology. New York, 1962.
Walton, J. H., Covenant: God's Purpose, God's Plan. Grand Rapids, 1994.
Watson, W. G. E/N. Wyatt (eds.), Handbook of Ugaritic Studies. Leiden, 1999.
Weinfeld, M., The Promise of the Land: The Inheritance of the Land of

Canaan by the Israelites. Berkely/Los Angeles/Oxford, 1993.

Wellhausen, J., Die Composition des Hexateuch und der historischen Bücher des Alten Testament (4th ed.). Berlin, 1899.

Wellhausen, J., Prolegomenon zur Geschichte Israels. Berlin/New York, 2001.

Wiesle, E., Gates of the Forest. New York, 1966.

Wilson, S., Related Strangers: Jews and Christians 70-170 C. E. Minneapolis, 1995.

Wilson, T. A., The Curse of the Law and the Crisis in Galatia: Reassessing the Purpose of Galatians (WUNT 2. Reihe 225). Tübingen, 2007.

Wretlind, D. O., Shekels, Dollars & Sense: A Biblical Theology of Financial Stewardship. Victoria, 2006.

Wright, N. T., The New Testament and the People of God. Minneapolis, 1992.

2. 3 ARTICLES

Alaba, S. O., "Improving the Standard and Quality of Primary Education in Nigeria: A Case Study of Oyo and Osun States" (IJCDSE. Vol. 1, Issue 3). September 2010.

Airoldi, N., "La cosiddetta 'decima' israeltica antica," Bibl 55 (1974), 179-210.

Baden, J. S., "The Violent Origins of the Levites: Text and Tradition": In Levites and Priests in Biblical History and Tradition, M. Leuchter/J. M. Huton (eds.) SBL 9, (2011), 103-106.

Barnard, J. A., "Anti-Jewish Interpretations of Hebrews: Some Neglected Factors," Melilah, Vol. 11 (2014), 25-52.

Barrick, W. D., The Mosaic Covenant, TMSJ 10/2 (Fall 1999), 213-232.

Barth, G., "Matthew's Understanding of the Law" In: Tradition and

Interpretation in Matthew. G. Barth et al (eds.) NTLi (trans. by P. Scott). 1963, 58-164.

Beckwith, R. T., "The Unity and Diversity of God's Covenants," The TynB 38 (1987), 93-118.

Begg, C. T., "The Golden Calf Episode According to Pseudo-Philo": In M. Vervenne, Studies in the Book of Exodus (1996), 577–94.

Boloje, B. O/Groenewald, A., Perspectives on Priests' Cuiltic and Pedagogical Malpractices in Malachi 1:6-2:9 and their Consequent Acts of Negligence. JS 22/2 (2013) 376-408.

Brown, S., "The Matthean Community and the Gentile Mission." NT 22 (1980), 193-221.

Bruce, F. F., "Christianity Under Claudius," BJRL 44 (March 1962): 309-326.

Busenitz, I. A., Introduction to the Biblical Covenants: The Noahic Covenant and the Priestly Covenant, TMSJ 10/2 (Fall 1999) 173-189.

Clendenen, E.R., "Malachi" in: E. R. Clendenen/R. A. Taylor (eds.), Haggai, Malachi (NAC 21A). Nashville, 2004, 203–464.

Cook, M. J., "The Gospel of John and the Jews," RvExp 84 (Spring 1987).

Cranfield, C. E. B., "St Paul and the Law," SJTh 17 (1964).

Dae-Ikang, The Royal Component of Melchizedek in Hebrews. Perichoresis Vol. 10. Issue 1 (2012), 95-124.

Elliot-Binns, L. E., "Some Problems of the Holiness Code." ZAW 65 (1955), 26-40.

Emerton, J. A., "The Site of Salem, the City of Melchizedek (Genesis xiv 18)." In Studies in the Pentateuch, ed. J. A. Emerton VT.S 41(1990), 45-71.

Fitzmyer, J. A., "The Aramaic Qorbän Inscription from Jebel Hallet et-Turi and Mk 7:11/Mt 15:5," Essays on the Semitic Background of the New Testament. London (1971), 93-100.

----------, "'4QTestimonia' and the New Testament", Essays on the Semitic Background of the New Testament. London, 1971, 59-89.

Fredriksen, P., "Why Should a 'Law-Free' Mission mean a 'Law-Free' Apostle?" JBL 134, no.3 (2015), 637-650.

----------, P., "Judaizing the Nations: The Ritual Demands of Paul's gospel." NTS 56, (2010), 232-52.

Fredriksen, P., Did Jesus Oppose the Purity Laws? Bible Review XI.3 (1995), 18-25.

Goulder, M., "Matthew's Vision for the Church," A Vision for the Church: Studies in early Christian Ecclesiology. M. Bocknuehl/M. B. Thompson (eds.). Edinburgh, 1997, 19-32.

Fleddermann, H., "A Warning about the Scribes (Mk 12.37b-40)," CBQ 44 (1982), 61-67.

Heltzer, M., "On Tithe Paid in Grain at Ugarit," IEJ 25 (1975).

Jagersma, H., "The Tithes in the Old Testament," In: Remembering All the Way, Oudtestamentische Studien 21. Leiden, 1981.

Knohl, I., "The Law of Sin-Offering of the Holiness School," Tarbiz 59 (1989-90), 1-9.

Knohl, I., "The Priestly Torah Versus the Holiness School: Sabbath and the Festivals," HUCA 58 (1987), 65-117.

Levin, S., "The More Savory Offering: A Key to the Problem of Gen 4:3-5," JBL 98 (1975), 85.

Lewis, J. P., "The Offering of Abel (Gen 4:4): A History of Interpretation," JETS 37/4 (December 1994) 481-496.

Nielsen, E., "The Levites in Ancient Israel," In: Law, History and Tradition: Selected Essays by Eduard Nielsen. Cophenhagen, 1983, 71-81.

North, R., "Eser, sr, maáSër," TDOT XI. 404-409.

Peets, H., "Die Rolle des Erziehungswesens in der englischen Kolonialpolitik in Nigeria," In: H. N. Weiler (ed.) Erziehung und

Politik in Nigeria. Freiburg (1964), 80-160.

Preuss, H. D., "bô," TDOT, II.20-49.

Rehm, M. D., "Levites and Priests" ABD 4 (1992), 297-310.

Rengstorf, K. H., "Korban, Korbanas," TDNT 3, 860-66.

Rivkin, E., "Defining the Pharisees: The Tannaitic Sources," HUCA 40-41 (1969-1971): 205-249.

----------, "Scribes, Pharisees, Lawyers, Hypocrites: A Study in Synonymity," HUCA 49 (1978), 135-142.

Rudolph, D. J, "Yeshua and the Dietary Laws: A Reassessment of Mark 7:19b," Kesher 16 (Fall, 2003), 97-98.

Rudolph, D. J., "Jesus and the Food Laws: A Reassessment of Mark 7:19b," EQ 74:4 (2002), 291-311.

Schiffman, L. H., "Priestly and Levitical Gifts," The Provo International Conference on the Dead Sea Scrolls: Technological Innovations, New Texts, and Reformulated Issues Vol. 30 (1999), 480-496.

Schmid, K., "Israel am Sinai: Etappen der Forschungsgeschichte zu Ex 32– 34 in seinen Kontexten," in Gottes Volk am Sinai: Untersuchungen zu Ex 32-34 und Dtn 9-10 (ed. Köckert, M./Blum, E.), WGT 18. Gütersloh, 2001.

Schrenk, G. "δικαιοσύνη" TDNT II.

Smith, W. R., "Sacrifice," Encyclopedia Britannica, 9th ed., (Vol. 21), 132-138.

Smoler, L./Aberbach, M., "The Golden Calf Episode in Postbiblical Literature," HUCA 39 (1968), 91–116.

Sprinkle, J. M., Law and Narrative in Exodus 19–24, JETS 47/2 (June 2004), 235–52.

Tate, M. E., "Tithing: Legalism or Benchmark?" RvExp 70/2 (Spring 1973), 153-161.

Turner, C. H., "Parenthetical Clauses in Mark," JTS 26 (1925), 145-156.

Waldman, N. M., "Some Notes on Malachi 3:6; 3:13; and Psalm 42:11," JBL 93 (1974), 543-549.

Watts, J. J., "Aaron and the Golden Calf in the Rhetoric of the
    Pentateuch," JBL 130/ 3 (2011), 417–430.
Weinfield, M., "Berith—Covenan t vs. Obligation," TDOT 2:255-256.
Wendland, "Linear and Concentric Patterns in Malachi," 113.

2. 4. INTERNET SITES

Boloje, B. O. and Groenewald, A., Hypocrisy in stewardship: An ethical
reading of Malachi 3:6–12 in the context of Christian stewardship.
Available at
http://www.hts.org.za/index.php/HTS/article/view/2086/4649.

ABOUT THE AUTHOR

Rowland Onyenali, CMF is a Catholic priest. He is a member of the eastern province of the Claretian missionaries in Nigeria. He holds BPhil from the Urban University, Rome, a B. A in religion from the University of Nigeria, Nsukka, an M.A in Theology from the Duquesne University, Pittsburg, USA as well as an M.A in Religious Education and a Ph.D in New Testament Exegesis from the Julius Maximillian Universität in Würzburg, Germany. Currently he teaches at the Spiritan International School of Theology (SIST), Attakwu, Enugu State. He is also a visiting lecturer at the Seat of Wisdom Seminary, Ulakwo, Imo State and at the Claretian Institute of Philosophy (CIP), Nekede, Imo State.

His major publications include:

The Covenant God: A Moral Exhortation. Lagos, 2006.

The Trilogy of Parables in Matthew 21:28-22:14 from a Matthean Perspective. Frankfurt, 2013.

Appraising the Nigerian Problem through Education and Religious Dialogue: A Cognitive Approach. Frankfurt, 2013.

Let Our Women Give Birth like the Hebrew Women: Random Musings on Christian Prayer and Praxis. Lagos, 2014.